BOBBIE ABBOTT

BOBBIE ABBOTT

WITH THE TRUE LONDONER
DANNY ANTHONY

CONTENTS

To Bobbie

The times fly past gathering pace each day, and we've stuck together in some old fashioned way; I love you now as from the start; how well you know this truth, Just to hold your hand in mine can still renew my youth.

. . . Danny

Me, aged 1, with my brother, Patsy, standing

Chapter 1

Southend, 1947

We were on our way to Southend, not to see The Kursaal, paddle or to eat jellied eels, but to deliver beer. Southend at that time, in 1947, was to Londoners the place to visit and whether you went by bike, train, bus, coach, or pleasure steamer from Millwall via the Isle of Dogs, stopping to pick-up at Tilbury, you always ended up at the end of the pier.

At weekends, high days and holidays it was bustling with excitement, kiss-me-quick hats and the sound of the Laughing Sailor at the entrance of the pier.

I was with my Uncle Gus waiting to be picked up outside Mile End Hospital, Bancroft Road, just a few streets away from Charrington's Brewery.

The lorry pulled up already loaded from the night before with crates and barrels of beer and, after a few words with the driver, we climbed on the back in between the crates, with a tarpaulin over our heads.

Before I'd jumped on the back of the lorry, I noticed there were two other people in the cab along with the driver. They were the drayman and his daughter Roberta. My uncle's name was Joseph Abbott; I never knew why they called him Gus, but he was no relation of the drayman Tom Abbott.

It was in the school holidays and with it being quite a long trip, and the idea of going to Southend, I jumped at the offer of going along for the ride. Although we never exchanged words all that day – we were only 8 years old – destiny had already decided that Roberta and I would meet again.

I was born in Barnsbury, Islington, and lived in Plender Street, Camden Town, NW1. She, Roberta, lived in Knapp Road, Bow E3. My dad, Charles Anthony, was in the army during the war. He was a Long-Range Sniper (Royal Artillery) at one time stationed in Primrose Hill with our version of Big Bertha (a very large gun which the Germans had in World War Two). They still have the gun crater there.

My father's mother's name was Murphy which accounts for our Irish names: Mary, Patrick, Eileen, me (Danny), Doreen, Terry (who died at the age of 14), Brian and Joseph. She used to have a flower stall in Drury Lane, W1, but Granny Murphy died before I was born. Grandfather Anthony was a big fat man, and his work was minding the horse and carts at the old fruit and veg market in Covent Garden, which was in the heart of London near to Drury Lane's Royal Opera House.

His job was telling the traders where to park and leave their carts, and directing the porters in loading the correct carts. His only income was from tips off of the traders. If you did not tip him well enough you were never allowed to park or you were parked too far away.

As we made our way to Southend the roads were quite clear. The back of the brewer's lorry seemed like a great adventure and Southend a million miles away. I should point out that I'd never travelled in a lorry or car before; the only place I'd ever been was Preston in Lancashire when we were evacuated, a week after Dunkirk in June 1940, and I was too young to remember much of it.

The little I did remember, prompted by my mum and older brothers and sisters, was that as we arrived at Kings Cross station, L.N.E.R. (London and North Eastern Railways), there were hundreds of soldiers and sailors milling around with bandages wrapped around them, some being led, others being carried on stretchers, with nurses and doctors moving from man to man. Apparently they were being loaded on to the same train that we were on and, as we found out later, being distributed around the country to any hospital that could accommodate them and the best way to do that was by train.

Those wonderful steam engines were the quickest way of getting our heroes attended to. On route to Preston, Lancaster, we stopped at three or more stations where carriages were unloaded and wounded men were put into ambulances.

Then off we would go again until finally that powerful old engine, with smoke bellowing out of its funnel, came to a halt at the station. We had arrived at Preston. There we all sat on a bench at the station, Mum, Mary, Patsy, Eileen, me and Doreen the baby. I could never find out if we paid our train fares or whether we had labels stuck or tied on our lapels. All I can remember is getting into trouble after eating my brother's half of a bag of crisps. His half was on the top and I had to eat his half to get to my half which was on the bottom.

We were all taken to a large country house. Its owner was Lord Derby who owned most of the land around the county. We were fed, bathed and put to bed. Sometime later the authorities gave us a house to live in, 177 Plungington Road.

It's still there; my sister Eileen went back and photographed it. I don't know how long we were there but I will never forget that long train journey, looking out of the windows, hearing the whistle blow, and watching England's beautiful countryside, the miles of green fields, and following the Regents Canal winding its way into the Grand Union Canal which stretches from the Thames at Limehouse all the way up to Preston, and into the river Ribble.

Apart from the train, the only things I'd ever ridden on was a pair of skates with two wheels missing, a bike without a chain and saddle (which used to make your eyes water!) and a go-cart with no 'go' in it.

Well, that's not quite true. Once a year we were treated to a bus ride, the old number 68 from Camden Town to Somers Town, but we had to walk home. Like most people living in our area of London, my family were mostly very poor and only had a radio, or wireless as we called it then.

But because we had no electricity in our house, we had to hire accumulators (a thick glass container roughly the size of a small car battery, filled with acid). You would have to get it recharged every time it ran out of juice (or power) which was really frustrating, especially when it ran out halfway through a boxing match and you never knew who'd bloody won the fight. As I've already said, we didn't have electricity in our house, only gas. This was only for lighting purposes; there were gas pipes in every room, placed just above head height (unless you were a bloody giant).

An open fire, with a built-in-oven, did all the cooking. The fuel used for cooking was coal and coke, and of course this was also our only way of heating, which we could never afford. We used anything that would burn, and at night before you went to bed, you'd close down the air flaps as we called them; one under the fire gate and one up the chimney, put all potato peelings and anything else on top of the fire, pour a little water and damp down for the night, hoping that the heat of the fire would slowly keep the fire going all through the night. Come morning we'd open the air flaps, rake out the ashes and 'God willing' the fire would still be alight.

The fire was the most important thing in the house. We had a copper boiler in the scullery but it had never worked, so we relied on the fire for everything. Hot water was never wasted. The kettle was always filled up, we never wasted heat. It had to go a long way; eight kids, mum and dad, all that washing, bathing in a long tin bath, the washing up, cleaning and making tea. All done with one kettle – a bloody miracle!

There was not one of us, at one time or another, who had not burnt their hand taking the kettle off the fire. And of course, because we had no electric or gas stove, the fire was always a light, summer and winter.

I can just imagine all us kids in the middle of winter, in the days when it seemed to stay icy for months, all sitting, mostly on the floor laid over with old newspapers (easy to keep clean, but always cold), we'd wrap anything around us to keep warm. Our mum would tell us stories, the younger ones would play cricket, (no, not with a bat and ball, with a book).

We'd open the book at any page and look at the first letter of each line. If it was the letter B, then that was a wicket taken. B = Bowled, C = Caught, RO = Run-out, S = Single, F = Four runs and so on. We never had rain stopped play although many a night bad light stopped play when we could no longer read the words in the book and, alas, had no money for the gas meter – that's if all the gas mantles were not broken. Bed time was the worst fear – freezing cold rooms and beds We always had bricks in the oven, which we would wrap rags around, and put them into the beds to warm us up. That fire was priceless. Of course nobody had TVs, videos, phones, double glazing, central heating, fitted carpets, bathrooms or – ha-ha – en-suites! We all had outside loos and most people had never been abroad, except with the armed forces.

The beach at Tower bridge, hop picking or, if you were lucky, Southend was where we went on our holidays.

It had not been two years since the war had ceased. London was cleaning up, there was bomb sites and burnt out shops, buildings, schools, factories and houses with debris everywhere you looked. And we still had ration books for clothing and food, in fact we had meat once, but I put down my fork to blow my nose and somebody thought I was finished and nicked it.

I must get back to Roberta, the girl sitting up front in the driver's cab. A good looking girl, she was the youngest of five children. To think that when I first saw her we were outside the Mile End Hospital, Bancroft Road and 23 years later she returned to that same hospital to give birth to our lovely daughter, Deborah. Destiny is a funny thing, full of coincidences and surprises.

Roberta was born in 8 Knapp Road, Bow E3 – everybody called her

Bobbie. Her grandfather, Tom Abbott, a seaman who sailed on many a fine ship from 1882 to 1895 – the Hotspur, Northampton Stork, Duncan, Alexandra, Helicon, and the Duke of Wellington to name a few – traced his origins back to Bury-St-Edmonds.

Her dad, Tom Abbott, met her mum, Margaret, when he was in the navy and they started courting. When they decided to get married her parents objected; they did not think Tom was good enough for their daughter.

Margaret's father was an architect and bridge builder – quite well off – and a respectable mason. He had given Margaret, being their only child, a proper education; good schooling, piano lessons, singing lessons, and she had on occasions played and sang at his Ladies' nights.

However, they knew nothing about true love and would not give Margaret her birth certificate, which she needed to get married. Tom and Margaret would not be put off; they went to Somerset House and found out, to her amazement, that the people she had always known as her parents, Mr & Mrs Caswell, had never had any children. They were in fact her uncle and aunt, who had taken her on holiday when she was young, and moved out of this country where they could not be traced. They returned some time later to Poplar, E14, with everybody assuming that Margaret was theirs.

Margaret Caswell was really Margaret Llewellyn. She contacted her family in Merthyr Tydfil and discovered she had a brother and three sisters. She soon became Mrs Abbott – without the blessing of Mr & Mrs Caswell – and moved over to Bow, London E3.

My family, the Anthony's, came from Somers Town, Euston, and when mum and dad got married they moved around a lot; Charlton Street, Somers Town, Copenhagen Street, up to Torino Avenue N1 and then Regina Street and Plender Street in Camden Town, NW1.

My mum's name was Helena Holmes or Nelly to her friends. Her father was a bailiff and, rumour has it, he even evicted his own family. He put all their belongings on the street but let them back in at night. He was a very strict man.

On the few occasions we saw him we sat up straight on the chairs and were frightened to move. My mum had left home at an early age to live with her gran because he was so strict. Her mother's (our gran's) name was Ginny Holmes, and she lived in St Mary's flats in Drummond Street, Euston. She lived to a ripe old age and could always be found having a drink in the Lion and Lamb Pub on the corner of Drummond Crescent, where you could always rely on her getting up to sing.

Mum had three sisters and two brothers but we were never really close to them. My dad's family, The Anthony's, were spivs; we were quite close to them so I suppose we know their bad ways, as well as their good. From as far back as I remember we lived in Camden Town, NW1.

I seem to remember Regina Street as an ordinary, quiet London Street with the Webb's, James, Cronings, Wilsons, Ashbolt, Humphries and Fry's to name a few. I can still see, feel and hear the sound of music coming out of the open windows (oh yes, the doors and windows were always left open, even if you went out, most doors with a bit of string through a hole to open the door) whilst walking up the street to play with a friend on a Sunday morning. I must have been about 6 or 7 years old.

I'm sure it was family favourites, and 50 years later, whilst on holiday in France, at a place called Castillonnès in the Dordogne area, we were strolling down this lovely little boulevard, and the first floor windows of the house were open. I stopped and said to Bobbie and Debbie, 'Listen to that music, feel the atmosphere. This reminds me of Regina Street, when I was a small boy.' I really expected my old mate, Roy Ellis, to come running up the road.

My earliest memories were of Regina Street, NW1, with Pratt Street at the top end, and Plender Street at the bottom.

The bakers were on the corner of Pratt Street opposite the large gates of the gardens, which was a small park between Pratt Street and Camden Street. Most of the kids played full time cricket or football matches in the street; there were hardly any interruptions from traffic and when a lorry came along us kids used to hang on to the back up to the corner, where it had to slow down for us to jump off, although I can vaguely remember falling off and hurting my chin.

Another injury I remember was once, when playing William Tell, I stood with my back to the air-raid shelter with a corrugated tin sheet in front of my body and face. The marksman – a girl of 6, Brenda Fry – could see the apple on my head, with the tin sheet in front of me. I waited and waited (patience was never my strong point even then), then took the sheet away to tell her to hurry up. I've still got the scar, dead centre of my forehead.

We moved around the corner to 14 Plender Street next door to the butchers and opposite the Pars Head pub. The song I remember the best was *Now is the Hour*, possibly because every night at 10 o'clock closing time the landlord, Jack Carnaby, used to usher all his clients outside, and the last song was *Now is the Hour* which seemed to have no ending. We would drift off in our sleep with the words in our minds.

Our mum was known as the woman with all the kids. She used to sell our clothes rations allowance to get food, and even with all us young children, she was out working. It was no wonder that she died at the early age of 59.

How she struggled with all us kids. When the sirens sounded she would get us all together and we would run for our lives down Bayham Street, into Crowndale Road, past The Mornington Crescent post office, across Overshot Street to Mornington Crescent underground station. There we were, all huddled together and not knowing what might happen, until morning. When the *All Clear* was sounded we would drag our weary bodies to the surface, into the sunlight and thank God we were still alive. I can still remember the sound of the Doodlebugs, seeing the searchlights, hearing the guns and coming out of the station, seeing the statue of Richard Cobden and a line of fire engines up and down Camden High Street.

The Bedford Theatre was partially hit, and the shops and houses next to it practically razed to the ground. On the other side, nearer to the station, the roof of the Camden Palace where the famous Harry Houdini appeared was still alight. We must have had some of his magic to survive it all, but we got through.

The underground was not always the safest place to be. In September 1940 Marble Arch Station, W1, took a direct hit that killed twenty people. A month later a bomb exploded above Balham Station, South London, damaging water and sewerage pipes which flooded the tunnel where hundreds of people were sheltering from the air-raids. 68 people perished with many more injured.

In the centre of the City of London, Bank Station took a direct hit which killed 56 people, who again thought they were absolutely safe sheltering underground. And without a single bomb falling, 173 people died at the Bethnal Green Station, with many more injured through panic – stumbling down the stairs – running from what they thought were bombs (but later found to be new anti-aircraft guns at nearby Victoria Park), packing into the entrance and trampling on top of victims who had fallen.

From September 1940 to May 1941, the Luftwaffe bombed London and Britain – after unmercifully crushing six countries. Of course we went to

Preston in 1940 just after Dunkirk, but we returned home in the middle of an air raid. Our propaganda was so good we believed it ourselves. I can always remember my mum saying in later years – concerning the first night back when the air-raids had started, there was guns going off, searchlights, the noise of the aircraft engines, whistling bombs, explosions, fire engines – 'If that was winning,' she said, 'I glad we were not losing.'

I was 10 months old when the war began and 6 years old when it ended. I'm glad I can just remember the last year. Although the fighting had stopped, the battle had just begun. Instead of the fear of being blown up, Britain was on its knees; there were 45,000,000 people to feed, thousands to re-house, the hospitals that had not been blown up were over-crowded, there were factories to re-build, and we needed time to grieve. Add to all that the price of peace. I can remember in the early days at school, not wanting to go and getting into a fight because some kid laughed at my shoes – he said they were girl's shoes. I think my sister and I shared them; I wore them to school one day and she wore them the next which meant we had every other day off, so it wasn't all bad. I could not do woodwork because we were asked to take in our own hammer and saw and we did not own any tools whatsoever in our house. If we had maybe, just maybe, someone would have mended the window and we would not have had to wake up with snow actually settling on our heads. It was colder inside the house than out and I forget how many slept in one bed, but the last one in tied the rope up, to stop anybody falling out.

We shared it with the bugs. Hitler would have done us all a favour if he'd blown it up whilst we were in Preston, but I'm glad he didn't really, because we had an old man living up-stairs in 14 Plender St, all on his own.

We were not sure if he knew there was a war on because he was stone deaf. He lived all on his own; no money for gas or lighting and, like most families, he did all his cooking on an open fire.

One day my dad decided to clean the chimney. Because we had no chimney sweeping rods or brushes we used to get a sack, a brick, and a length of rope, tie the rope around the middle of the sack with the other end around the brick. Then we'd drop the brick down the chimney, go downstairs into the room and look for the brick. If we'd put it down the correct chimney we'd just pull the sack through. As easy as cleaning your rifle barrel! But this time he got the wrong chimney. Next thing we saw was the old man standing there, covered in soot, still holding his frying pan with a load of soot mixed up with his tomatoes.

It was not all doom and gloom. Somehow we got invited to Bertram Mills Circus at Olympia. I think it was arranged through the post office at Crowndale Road, Mornington Crescent – Mum used to work there at Christmas. There were the days when we had egg powder from out of the food parcels we received from our Commonwealth countries and I'd like to take this opportunity to thank them.

Those were the days when there were 24 hours in a day, when you had no time-consuming television, when you queued up for the football results outside Mornington Crescent station, every Saturday night. I'll always remember the paper man's name – it was Ginger Parkington, an ex-QPR player. He'd shout out 'Star, News, or Standard! Classified results' and would sell out in minutes. You'd stand and watch them turn the trolley buses around, while waiting for the next delivery.

The buses would stop outside the Camden Palace facing Euston. A man would reach up with a long pole and take the supply lines – two long arms reaching out the roof of the bus – off of the electric cable and use the battery to drive the bus around the Richard Cobden statue, then reconnect the arms and proceed in the opposite direction towards Camden Town station.

I would stand in the queue and get my 4 or 5 papers and take them back to Plender Street market and hand them round to the stall holders. I could rely on getting some fruit and veg for going and, of course, I'd help them to put their stalls away in the bottom of Camden Mews, some ex-stables turned into lockups. I suppose now they are mews flats.

My older brother Patsy used to work for Jarvis's fruit and veg stall. He also used to bring home fruit and veg, and added them to the bacon bones brought from Sainsbury's bacon counter and Mum's bread pudding; I suppose we were well fed. This is all we had when the food parcels stopped.

Camden Town was an area already crowded with different nationalities, being near to four main line stations, Kings Cross, Euston, St Pancreas, and Paddington – people from all over the U.K. would settle near and around the stations. People would also come from all round the world, via the ports to London. In the 1920s the Irish came and built the Black Cat building.

The Greek and Cypriots settled there – Makarious had his arms factory beneath a church in the crypt in Camden Street and Pratt Street, NW1. Just along the road, off Royal College Street, Bain Street was one of the first (if not the first) to have racial trouble which made the papers in 1947/48.

My mum grew up in Somers Town which is in Euston near to Kings Cross. She lived with her family up the alley off Little Drummond Street. Nowadays Charlton Street antique market is at one end of the alley, with Drummond Street at the other end.

I can still recall how well she spoke about our dad when they were young, how she would walk out holding his arm and felt the envy of all the other girls. She described his good looks, with his dark hair parted down the middle like George Raft; he must have been quite a catch. My dad was quite well known in Somers Town, mainly for his boxing abilities. He kept himself very fit and never started to drink alcohol until he was 37.

My mum was only five feet tall, but was quite a formidable person and could turn her hand to doing most things. At one time she made wreaths, and flower arrangements. She would take home work.

One job we had – I say we because all us kids would try to help – was for a firm down Euston Road called Bassett's Liquorish Allsorts. They got mum to collect four large cardboard boxes filled up with cardboard tubes. Mum would wrap and stick on the labels, sealing one end. She would then pack all the tubes back into the large boxes and return them to the factory to be filled with sherbet and a stick of liquorish. If my memory serves me right they were called Sherbet Dabs.

Anyhow, we stayed up half the night putting them together and sticking on the labels. We packed them into the boxes, loaded them on the pram, and pushed it all the way down to Euston. Little old Mum carried them up the stairs, and a short time after, came down the stairs, crying and swearing. She told me they would not pay her any money, because the ****** things had all stuck together.

Another job she had was at Christmas, working with our Aunt Kate, delivering letters and parcels. They nearly came a cropper one year when my uncle Bill started talking to them and took their attention away from the post office lorry long enough (we think) to give one of his dubious friends time to help himself to some parcels. They shouted after the thief but he was never caught.

One of my fondest memories is of our days out in Regent's Park. I don't know if my memory plays tricks but it always seemed that we had long hot summer days.

There we all were, mum and at the time, in 1946/47, seven kids, Mary

15, Patsy 13, Eileen 11, me 7, Doreen 5, our Terry 4, and Brian the baby. Trekking up to Regent's park, loaded up with bottles of water, cheap lemonade or sherbet powder and bread and dripping, (juice and fat from meat – yes, you could actually buy it! – And a bag of broken biscuits. We'd have a ball and played rounders or cricket, swapping picture cards from cigarette packets, an old bicycle wheel without spokes to use as a hoop, and the girls always seemed to have a piece of rope for skipping.

We'd pick up 5 stones and play gobs. Of course the park had swings, roundabouts and a sandpit, and plenty of open spaces to run and play.

They were long, happy, sunny days. I look back with fond memories on my early days in Camden Town. The house we lived in, 14 Plender Street, was knocked down years ago, but it had been a really fine house and obviously had been occupied by some rich people. Only having gas lighting, it must have been built in the 1800s. It had high ceilings, with shutters inside the lead-weighted sash windows, and small balconies with cast-iron fronts, stopping you from falling out.

The large ceiling roses, being cast on to two lengths of 4"x2" pieces of wood, were nailed to the ceiling joists. All the ceilings and walls were plastered with wooden laths and lime and horse hair plaster. Two large doors opening into the back room separated it from the front parlour.

Both rooms had skirting boards, dado rails (or high-backed chair rails), and picture rails with the freeze above and ornate coving.

Most walls in the house, were covered in thick lincrusta wall paper below the dado rails with lovely (I appreciate them now) cast iron fire surrounds. Our bedroom walls had been papered with the famous willow patterned wallpaper. It was many years after that I heard the willow pattern story and remembered it was all over our bedroom walls.

There were two fig trees in the back yard with the outside toilet nearby at the bottom of the garden / yard, and each year the pipes in the loo would freeze up – they had more holes than a sheet of peg-board.

If toilet rolls had been invented, we never saw any. Usually there were yesterday's newspapers, torn into squares with a bit of string hanging from the pipes, or tied to the chain from the overhead water system.

Of course, there were no outside lights en route to the loo or inside the toilet. Most people had a chamber pot, or a *goes under*, a pot that goes under the bed.

As rumours would have it, some scrawny little angelic looking boy could be seen and heard sitting on the loo, clapping his hands and singing

Deep in the heart of Texas. My singing talents did not stop there; I somehow got to sing in a church choir but got thrown out for hitting a girl that I thought was a boy. I now think that I know the difference although sometimes you can't be too sure.

St. Pancras Gardens was quite near to where we lived and, whatever way you approached it, you would have to go under a bridge and pass hundreds of arches. In those days the arches were used as stables or lockups.

Early every morning you would see hundreds of horses and carts making their daily rounds delivering coal, milk or anything that could be sold from off the back of a cart. Life was good if you were a tomato grower, with tons of horse manure piled up in the road or around the horses' water troughs – those long large granite troughs with a hand pump to top it up with water – could be seen everywhere. I wonder how many are still around.

Back to St. Pancras Gardens and its lovely old church. We had to go back near to it years after to register the death of our mum. Every corner we turned gave us sad and even wonderful memories of my early days in Camden Town. I rarely go there nowadays, it hurts too much.

One lasting memory of Plender Street was the lovely Sunday mornings, watching the gathering of boys and men meeting on the corner of Bayham Place getting ready to walk to Regents Park.

As you approached the park, you could see dozens of other groups converging on the large open playing fields, all on foot (hardly a car in sight), with the zoo running along the back of the wide open cricket pitches. I wonder what the animals thought when they were awakened by the shouting out of *'How's that?'* by those men all dressed in white, knocking about a piece of leather (it looked like a piece of the poor chap who used to be in the cage next door). Of course in those days the batsmen would walk if they were given out – not like today, where they might try to sue the umpire for unfair dismissal.

Regent's Park was not only known for its sports facilities and the zoo, the lake was well known for its ducks and swans. Each year at Easter time there was the Horse and Cart parade which attracted thousands of people, and in the autumn we would collect conkers by the thousands.

Collecting was quite the thing to do then. All the cigarette packets, (Players, Weights, Turf, Craven A, and many more) usually had photos of famous footballers, cricketers, or other famous sportsman printed on the packets. There were so many different companies – everybody seemed to smoke, it might have been to steady their nerves. Following two World Wars it was no wonder all our nerves were in a state.

Funny thing though, our mum never smoked, just as well – she never had much money to buy cigarettes. She seemed always to be arguing with my aunts Katy and Betty, who used to get miserable and moody if they had no money for fags or betting. My aunt Kate was forever betting and she would treat me if I would run down to a Mr Franks who lived at the bottom of Bayham Place.

I would take a piece of paper with a bet written out and signed 'Rusty'. This was her code name, because in them days betting and gambling was illegal. I would pretend that I was knocking to see if his son Peter would come out and play and I would give Mr Franks the note and money. He either phoned the bet through to the track, or collected as many bets as he could and went to the track to place a bet.

If anybody won he would get a percentage of their winnings. I remember one day as I got to the house two policemen was questioning Mr Franks so I run back home. I was so frightened I told my aunt Kate that I gave Mr Frank the bet and money. Later on I owed up and told my mum what had happened and was not allowed to take any more bets.

Although we lived in a large house, only one room in the house had a fire burning because of the shortage of fuel – wood, coal, coke, or anything else that would burn – and we would all congregate in this one room trying to keep warm. 'Close that xxxx door, don't let the cold air in.' That sentence was used more than any other, and of course we had to be quiet if anybody knocked at the door such as the rent men, insurance men, or the tallymen. Even without being told, we grow up saying, 'Mummy said she ain't in' to anybody knocking at our door – and there she was hiding behind the door.

Returning to myself, I was being brought up in the family trade, spiving. From the early age of six I was a tipster. My uncle Bill acquired a John Bull printing kit. I would pick a horse I thought would win out of the papers and print it on a piece of paper and put it in an envelope, i.e. *Flash Gordon, 3 o'clock, Epson*.

Apparently I was quite lucky and my uncle became quite well known, and quite well drunk, as he exchanged, or traded, *his* tips for cash and drinks.

Another scam they got up to was at the time King George died. When it was thought he was dying, my dad and his brothers brought all the black paint and black ribbon they could get, and waited. Immediately the king died they approached all the shops on the funeral route and arranged to paint the black strips around the windows and pin the black ribbon to the front of their shops, as this apparently was the way of showing their respect.

To add to that scam, they broke into an empty shop on the funeral route and charged people to watch the funeral procession from the balconies, and even the roof.

I went to Richard Cobden school – infants and then juniors, up to the old 11 plus exams – where I must of done reasonably well, because they sent me to a new (at the time) school.

The idea was for 11 year olds who had some potential, to be prepared for Polytechnic school. I believe it had something to do with my sports abilities.

In them days I was lean, mean and could always easily get into school teams at football and cricket. I remember if we won a match we were treated to a cream bun and even to this day when I achieve something, I treat myself to a cream cake.

My uncle Bill was skint, and needed money to get to the races so he said to me, 'Come on, I need your help'. We walked down Plender Street, past Wilson's fruit & veg, McGuiness' salad and flower stall and past Pettit's, the paper shop, into Camden High Street. As we approached Mornington Crescent we saw a window cleaner's ladder, leather and bucket, outside a shop. The window cleaner had just left it. I suppose he'd gone to tea.

My uncle put the bucket and leathers into my hand, picked up the ladder and said to me, 'It's ok, he's a mate of mine, he said I could borrow them.'

Off we went, past the Black Cat, down Hampstead Road, past the Tolma cinema on to the Royal Free Hospital and on to Paddington where we stopped outside a shop.

In went Uncle Bill and after 10 minutes he came out, saying to the shopkeeper, 'It'll be alright, I'll leave my lad here, I'll be back in half an hour.' Then, as he passed me, he said, 'When I call you, leave the ladders and all that stuff, and come to me.'

In five minutes, as soon as the shopkeeper had some customers, my uncle called me, and I ran to him.

Being so young and innocent, I didn't know at the time that Uncle Bill had stolen the ladders, bucket and leathers, got some money up-front for the materials, and used me as a decoy. He walked away with the shopkeeper's money.

Nearly 50 years later I returned to the shop, (although it had changed to a hairdresser's) with Bobbie, to buy a wig.

Down hopping

Chapter 2

From Camden Town to Bow and down hopping

Camden has always had a History of culture. Everywhere you will see Blue Plaques on the wall, Charles Dickens lived here, George Orwell, Dylan Thomas lived here, Mary Shelly, author of *Frankenstein* was born here – she must have known my uncle (just a thought!) – and I do know that Madness, the cult band, lived here.

In them days Camden Town was a nice place to live. On Saturdays and Sundays it was very quiet, not a lot of traffic, and weekdays we had our rush hour (but it only lasted an hour). We often went to Regent's Park and could easily bunk off and go to the zoo.

I can remember walking round the park looking for empty lemonade bottles, which we could get the deposit back if we went to the right shops. I also spent many an hour walking four greyhounds all the way around the park; I was paid by a local greengrocer called Bill McCallan to give them daily exercise. He also took my sister Doreen, then about 6, to Weston-super-Mare in 1949, which I thought was somewhere abroad, a foreign country. (Geography was never my strong point).

Approaching the park from Park Street, there was a water fountain and as kids we would climb all over it. Behind the fountain there was a vast area covered with ash where the army from the barracks in Albany Road used to practice with their horses and gun carriages. On Sundays a large group of Irishman used to stand around in a circle, whilst two men would takes turns to punch each other. The first man punched the other and then it was the other man's turn, until one or the other could take no more. The men in the circle would bet on the outcome.

The Regent's Canal, which starts at Limehouse, E3, used to run at the back of the barracks and the large houses, under the fountain to the back of the zoo and wind its way up country, all the way up to Lancashire. When we were evacuated the train we were on ran next to the canal for miles.

My memory lets me down so I cannot tell you a lot about Preston. I know we stayed in a house in 177 Plungington Road, Preston, but I'm not sure how long we stayed there. Returning to London, we were back to Plender Street,

I seem to remember our landlord's name being Arthur Benibow, and I believe we had to move from Plender Street, NW1, to Bow, E3, which we did in 1950 because we had not paid the rent. Anyhow we moved into a house, 14 Hedworth Street, Bow, E3. We found the people there a lot different and mostly English. They were noticeably better off – I suppose having the docks, shipping and all its various off-shoots, plus the number of factories, there was plenty of jobs, for everybody.

In and around Whitechapel, Bethnal Green, and Limehouse there were 4 brewers: Taylor Walkers, Charringtons, Mann-Crossmans and Truemans.

In Bow and Bethnal Green there were the cabinet and furniture makers and in Whitechapel the machinists and dressmakers. I remember the crowds of machinists, just waiting around outside Whitechapel Bell Foundry in the hope of getting some full or part-time work. All around Whitechapel Road, down New Road to Commercial Road, there were thousands of sweatshops.

You could always see racks of dresses, skirts, slacks, being loaded onto vans. The Whitechapel Waste was one of the busiest markets in London. There were firms in abundance from Old Ford to Stratford, Bow to East India Dock Road, on to Canning Town and right the way up to Fords in Dagenham – a hive of industry.

Hedworth Street was a nice little street comprising 24 houses. Our house had three rooms up and three down, a small scullery and, of course, an outside toilet. We did have electricity (I told you they were posh in East London), but no bathroom.

The house looked over a large triangle of Nissan huts, and late in 1955, prefabs – built in Newcastle, brought down to London on the backs of large lorries, lifted off by crane and placed on paving stones.

The Nissan huts were arched shaped roofs of corrugated sheets, with chicken wire and plastered walls. They were put there to house the Italian prisoners of war and then to house homeless people temporary after the war. Friends of ours lived there right up to 1963.

The temporary prefabs lasted until the late 1980s, not entirely the government's fault, but people liked living in them and they were cheap to rent. Our next door neighbours were the Baldasaries – she had married one of the prisoners of war. Apparently the prisoners were allowed to stay in

England, after the war was over.

One night we had a lot of police and CID officers – who actually run through our house – and captured a neighbour four doors away named Paul Seaborne.

He'd escaped from Broadmoor prison. Later, in 1965, he helped Ronnie Biggs to escape from Wandsworth prison. He drove the van outside the prison walls and Ronnie Biggs jumped in and got away.

My schooldays in Bow were spent in Devon's Road School, which had joined up with Knapp Road Boy's School owing to the Knapp Road School having been razed to the ground by Herr Hitler's bombs. Devon's Road School was actually in Knapp Road, conveniently place right next door to 8 Knapp Road where Bobbie Abbott was born and still lived with her family. I attended that school from 1950 to 1954 and loved the school immensely. I played cricket and football in the playground daily, many a time kicking the ball into their garden, but still did not know Bobbie Abbott. I knew that one of the most popular girls in the neighbourhood lived there I would see her and her friends as I passed them on our way to school. I can never remember Bobbie looking my way.

Whilst still at school, life was hard. Money was very scarce but schooldays were happy, and to my recollection schoolwork and sports in East London was some way behind North London, or Camden, where I came from. Instead of being just average at 3Rs, I found myself among the top three in almost every subject, and by the time I was 13 I was playing both cricket and football for the under 15 first team. Just because I was smaller than the rest of the team at that time they called me Titch. Years later I walked into The Marquis of Devonshire, in Devon's Road, near to Bow Common Lane, and the landlord, Kenny Hughes, whom I had not seen for years said, 'Hello, Titch. What can I get you?' By this time I was six inches taller than him.

As I was saying, money was scarce so after school I got a job. Three nights a week I was making darts, and dart boards for Dickey Hood, the son of Jack Hood, "News of the World" darts champion. Dickey lived in Knapp Road and I went to school with his son, Brian.

To earn more money, when I was about twelve, I started up a coke round. This meant knocking on doors and asking people if they wanted any coke for their fires. In them days everyone had an open fire; the coalman delivered but coke was cheaper, so I would get some customers each Friday night. During the winter months, and at the crack of dawn on

Saturday mornings, you'd find me queuing up outside the gasworks in Bow Common Lane. My dad used to drink with the man who served the coke, so it was arranged if I gave the man a drink, he would fill up extra bags.

One of my best customers was Mrs Abbott, Bobbie's mum. I would deliver the coke (coal, not drugs!) to them every Saturday morning. I used to split my earnings 50/50 with my mum who needed every penny she could get. Usually I went to the pictures Saturday afternoon. Either the Ben Hur in Whitehorse Lane, or the Poplar cinema in Commercial Road. In the summer months, on Saturdays, I went to sell pickles at Watney Street market, E1 and Rathbone Street, Canning Town.

I worked for Teddy Snooks, a onetime boxer and later wrestler, at the Mile End Arena, which stood at the corner of Eric Street, and Mile End Road. Teddy was around just before the Krays came on the scene, when Curly King was running wild. Teddy knew my dad because both were boxers – my old man had to fight to pay the rent when they lived in Charlton Street, Somers Town, NW1. He had nearly 400 fights, 200 as a pro, but the purse was collated by the knobbings (or money thrown into the ring) after each fight. Teddy Snooks' brother, Philly, at that time a scrap metal and car dealer, used to take us down hopping in Paddock Wood, Kent, and Teddy –being a business man – soon found a way to make some money.

There were dozens of orchards in Kent, so I was sent scrumping for apples and my sister Mary made the toffee, Teddy had the van, so we got it all together and travelled around the Hop fields, selling toffee apples.

I'll never forget the place, Pearson Green, near to Paddock Wood.

Even now it has not changed, although the locals would not agree. Coming down from Paddock Wood station to the Elm Tree pub, take the road towards Mardon and pass the lane leading across the railway lines to Old Hayes Farm. Continue on down the lane until you come to Mays Farm on the left. You will see an old wooden gate leading to the hop huts. These were brick built with corrugated tin roofs. All the cooking was done on an open fire.

The first lesson was to keep your faggots dry (a faggot is a bundle of twigs and small branches) and well supplied. This meant nightly raids on your neighbour's supplies because, having a large family, the allocation of two faggots a day that we got was not enough.

So you'd stock up with faggots from day one, usually hiding them under your beds. Ha! Beds! Of course some posh hoppers used to take their own beds from home and even redecorate the hop huts better then the house we lived in, arriving by lorry, or walking from Paddock Wood station with a much as they could carry. The majority of hoppers I knew had hardly anything to bring with them and would arrive with prams loaded with blankets, pots and pans, and all the kids dragging old cases and boxes tied up with bits of string, and usually coming from the poorest parts of London.

My old mum loved it, out in the open air, away from the humdrum of the day to day battle of feeding us kids, away from the trap of the big cruel city, where there were no shops – she must have been sick of window shopping with no money to buy even the smallest item, or necessities. No luxuries – which word was not even in our dictionary at that time. In fact, we did not have a dictionary.

We used to get a lift down to hopping from Philly Snooks, whose family went to the same farm.

He would pick us up then go with the four other families to drop them off at different farms. Once pass Routon Hill, on to Seven Mile Lane, you started seeing the hop fields. Rows and rows of bines, strung up in groups of fours. We'd arrive at the huts, unload, and the foreman showed you to your huts. Mum would say who's sleeping where – Mike Tyson would not have argued with her, all 5ft nothing. Her word was law, and nobody touched her kids or else – she was fearless. Even my old man was frightened of her, but we all loved and respected her. By the way, she made the best bread pudding ever.

On the subject of food, I suppose you could say that we grew up as vegetarians. Meat was never on the menu, that's if you don't count bacon bones and the one time we did have a hare. But nobody ate it, or the chicken our Terry had.

He fattened it up for Christmas, but nobody could bring themselves to eat it. Anyhow the dinners we had down hopping was hotpot, that's if it wasn't raining which made cooking in the open air quite tricky – then it was cold pot! Most vegetable was quite cheap in the country, and what you couldn't afford to buy you would scrump.

The foreman, a Mr Plankard, looked after the farmer's interest. He would get everyone out of the huts and on to the hop fields as early as possible.

The funny thing was, you would pick the hop like mad, pulling down the bines, braking of a sprig and then removing the leaves before pulling the hops off between thumb and forefinger and dropping them into a large bin, that was 6ft long 2ft high, with canvass stretched between two lengths of wood, nailed to two tri-pods leaving handles at each end.

Getting a good run was important – the bigger hops filled the bins faster. The foreman, Mr Plankard, would shout out, 'Pull no more bines,' and everybody would make out they had not heard him, pulling a few more bines down until he spotted them. The reason being you could pick more hops whilst you would have to wait for the measurer to come round and dig his basket into the bin, take out one bushel of hops at a time, tip them into a poke (sack), mark your book and move on to the next bin.

Sometimes it was not known until days later just how much a bushel you would be paid for picking them.

At the weekend, on a Saturday morning, Mum would line up at the farmhouse for a sub out of what we had earned. Usually at weekends visitors would arrive from home. Saturday nights were spent up the Castle Pub at the top of Castle Hill, half a mile uphill all the way. You needed that drink by the time you reached the top.

All us kids would mess about outside and then, at closing time, out of the pub would come the mums and dads and they would start singing as we made our way down hill back to the hop huts where we would bank the fires up and listen to the oldies telling stories about their youth until the early hours of the morning. Then we made our way to bed, sleeping on the straw filled palliasse laid over bare boards.

On Sundays we would go for long walks, sometimes along the railway lines, for a bit of tree climbing, scrumping or fishing.

Looking back, I would love to do it all again, but back then the whole idea of going hopping was to pay the rent, and have some kind of holiday. Monday mornings, rain or shine, it was back to the hop fields for eight or nine hours a day, the smaller kids filling up apple boxes and tipping them into the bin.

We'd call out to the pole-puller – the man with the long pole with a hook on the end of it – to pull down the heads (tops) of broken bines tangled around the steel cables, which they tied the strings to, so that the hop bines would grow up, similar to a row of runner beans. At the end of the day, mum would tell me to run home, with one of my sisters, to light a fire, and start preparing the evening meal. After dinner there was all ways a game of rounders or football and the smaller kids would make up their own game.

Not a television, radio, stereo or computer in sight – how did we live without them? When it rained down hopping, and it usually did, the noise of the rain beating down on the tin roofs would keep you awake. Then the next morning there was the long trek up to the hop fields with mud up to your arm pits, and when you pulled the bines down, you'd get drenched.

But then the happy time again, when the sun came out and we'd all sit on the side of the bins, picking hops, singing away, laughing, joking and visiting the people on the other bins, mainly to see how many hops they'd picked. There was a lot of rivalry, on who picked the most hops.

Another thing that has stuck with me after all these years is the terrible taste of the hops on your fingers when you snatched a sandwich or apple. Of course the taste might have been the insecticides that they sprayed on the hops, but whatever, I still do not really like the taste of beer.

The last year that I went hopping they introduced this large machine which I believe ended the need for us hop pickers, and we was all made redundant.

We sometimes go back to look over that place and remember mum, sitting on the bin with all her kids around her, smiling and happy. I will always remember her saying some years later when she was ill, that all she wanted was to be remembered, once in a while after her death.

I told her not to be silly and promised her none of us would ever forget her, and I hope with the help of this book, the memory of our mum will last forever.

At the end of Hopping they used to hold a talent contest, I suppose it was the start of *Stars in your Eyes*. One year when Johnny Ray was top of the hit parade, we had half a dozen, budding Johnny Rays. Of course, Johnny Ray won.

It was enough to make you cry. Hopping had one drawback for me, you see, I liked to think that if we had not gone hopping, I might have become a professional footballer.

The trouble was that they always held the district trials whilst we were down hopping, so I never got picked for East London. I, along with 2,000,000 other lads, thought I was good enough but I never got picked for Tottenham for £20 a week. That's all they used to get before Jimmy Hill changed things and unlike today's players, I would not have played for Arsenal for £400 a week, even though they never asked me.

But I did have the honour to play for the Bus House, a local club in

Devon's Road, Bow E3. I remember it as the best club in the world, much better than the posh Eaton Manor club at Hackney Marshes.

The nearby Glucus Street off Devon Road, with its red cinder pitch, was our Wembley and would draw huge crowds of approximately 50 or 60 spectators to watch us play!

At one match, when there was still national service, the goalkeeper who apparently was AWOL from the army, was spotted by the MPs and ran off (faster than Cliff Jones), which left the goal empty, and the other side scored. I heard afterwards he was caught and played in goal for the prisoners.

The Frances Mary Bus House, to give it the correct name, was very well known, and had thousands of members of all ages.

As long as you liked sport you would be welcome to train in football, cricket, boxing, athletics and general keep-fit. Belonging to the Bus House was a major part of growing up. Even in those days we had celebrities visit the club to encourage us. I can remember the great McDonald Bailey, the fastest man on earth at that time, coming to the club. Everybody wanted to shake his hand just in case some of his magic would rub off. Across the road from the Bus House, was Kitson Pub, which was the pub that I brought my first pint of beer in. Next to the pub was Bramble House. A block of flats surrounded by a wall with piers, and in between the piers, covered by wire mesh, there were iron stretchers left over from the war.

Along the road was All Hallows Church, opposite the Lighthouse, round into Glucus Street, to the baths. Now and again, though not too often, we did have a bath, usually on a Saturday morning.

It was chaos in there; shouting, screaming, throwing things into each others baths, and of cause calling out for hot water in number five when you were in number six. The poor guy in number 5 laying there, not knowing, would get scalded with hot water, and he would row with the attendant, and then try to get his own back by doing the same to some other innocent victim.

My last year of school was spent at Elizabeth Barrett Browning Secondary Modern School in Southern Grove Mile End.

The whole of Knapp Road Boys School, all 130 of us, was moved to Southern Grove, which ordinarily was an all girls' school.

I left school without any qualifications at all. My dad got me a job with a drinking friend of his as an apprentice something to do with Auto Electrics.

The money was very low, mum needed more help, so I left and started work with a tarmac firm. Living in the heart of 'worksville' I could get a job anywhere; there was all the brewers, Bryant & May's Match Factory, Conway Stewart Pen Co., Oxo's, Clarnico Sweets, Asphalt Co, roofers, and pipe lagers, the Gas Board, the Water Board, and local councils. At one time or another I worked for all of them and many more. At one of my jobs I was a sugar boiler, making chocolate and toffee for a firm in Solbry Street near Southern Grove.

A certain Bobbie Abbott worked there but we never spoke to each other. We even went on a beano coach trip to Southend, but still without any communication.

Later I worked at the Excelsior Biscuit firm in Thomas Road. She worked there also, but I left not knowing her, (I suppose you could say this was not love at first sight). In fact it was approximately 13 years after we first went to Southend, (Bobbie up front with the driver, me and my uncle Gus on the back of the Charringtons lorry) that we first dated. My sister Doreen also worked with Bobbie at Excelsior's, and when I left she and Bobbie got quite friendly, and the next thing I knew was they had arranged a date.

One of my jobs, tarmacking and building roads, led me to Mill Hill Army (REME) Barracks in 1957/58. We were having a laugh at all the sqauddies and giving the drill sergeant a bit of stick. The sergeant said, 'Don't any of you ever come here if you're called up, I'll make your lives bloody misery.' And that's exactly what happened – one of the lad's within a few months, had been called up to do his national service. We knew he was coming, and arranged a guard of honour with the drill sergeant present, as a reception for him.

We all lined up with our picks and shovels on our shoulders and the sergeant stood at the end, with a grimace on his face.

About the same time that was happening, the country was on alert concerning The Suez Canal crisis. Hundreds of Lorries, jeeps, guns, etc. were being sprayed a yellowish colour with a large H on top.

I suppose so that they could be seen from above. I thought that I might finish up having a holiday in Egypt – as it turned out three years later, instead of joining the Camel Corps I became a foot soldier.

After the crisis and that job came to an end, I found myself working in Hainault, up near the Maypole and the Retreat Pub, which in them days was a lovely little country pub, a place to go for a quite drink. We were erecting a small playground, with swings and roundabouts, and every time we passed them Bobbie and Debbie would shout out. The playgrounds I built are still standing – good old English workmen! After that job I worked for a short time at Hornchurch airdrome.

At that time you could not get from Hornchurch to the Cherry Tree, Rainham. The Southend Road did not go in a straight line between the two towns because the airdrome cut the road in two, and I can still remember the G.I. Pub as it was before they altered it. I then went to work for the Forest Gate *Destruction* Co, it was really *Construction* but we were not very good. Being in building, especially the kind of work our construction firm did, meant travelling everywhere, all over the East End, and into Essex.

I worked on the London Hospital – I say *on*, because I worked on the roof – of course it was in the middle of winter and, obviously, we worked in boiler houses in flaming June!

We was stripping off lead from the roof (they knew all about it, all above board) and replacing the lead with a new idea called *Newrolite*. Anyhow, I nearly ended up in the hospital. We had to cut the lead up into small strips, fold them and put them in a large dustsheet. The idea was to lower the dustsheet, with the lead inside, down onto the back of the lorry.

We had a ginny wheel fixed to a tripod, made from three scaffold poles. So we lifted the sheet on to the parapet wall, the rope tied to the sack went around the wheel and through a rope guide, (that is a round bit of metal, just large enough to allow the rope to pass through) and I had hold of the rope.

Harry Smith (or H as we called him) a small man, but luckily enough a very strong man, was helping me. I must say he should have been a comedian. He could make a joke out of anything. As I hung onto the rope, he pushed the dustsheet, loaded with lead, over the parapet wall.

Well, the tripod wobbled and creaked; the wheel started to turn and down went the sheet. I hung on for grim death but the lower it went the heavier it got, and I started to rise from the ground. Harry saw what was happening and grabbed me around the waist and, like I said, always the joker, he said, 'If I let you go you'll go right through that little hole in the guide.'

We managed to get it on to the lorry below and learnt a good lesson concerning gravity. I nearly never made old bones, and talking of old bones, our next job was at John Knights the soap manufacturers in Silver

Town, opposite Tidell basin

Tidell Basin was at the end of the Royal Victoria docks and right next to it was two streets of houses. Every high tide the streets got flooded. Most of the houses at the lower end, owned a rowing boat – to my knowledge Steve Redgrave never lived there.

But back to John Knights which was next to Tate and Lyles, you could not miss it; just follow your nose, the smell of old bones could be smelt from miles away. The bone yard was stacked high regularly, with bones brought in from the knackers' yard, to be melted down and made into perfumed soap! In the bone yard, wild cats used to scare the living daylights out of you. They were horrible looking creatures like small sabre-toothed tigers, untamed, with nasty blood shoot eyes. Poor H was bitten by one and asked for danger money and, along with the rest of the gang of five, got it.

Of course his bite was entered in the accident book, which seemed to belong to (I put my hand on my heart and swear) David Jinks, Jinks by name and Jinx by nature. It was like his autobiography. It read, on so and so date, D Jinks, (dumper driver) was sent to hospital by his doctor with a suspected rupture, brought on by constant bumping up and down on the dumper seat.

He came back after two weeks, so I gave his a job helping the pipe fitter and he ended up in the accident book again.

He was working in a loft area above the toilets, putting in a bypass pipe, around a gas meter. It read, 'Whilst tightening up a nut, the spanner slipped and took the skin from off the back of his knuckles. He stood up and his foot went through the ceiling, bringing down plaster, (inconvenience, below) and cutting his leg. At the same time as he stood up, he cut his head.'

Another time he had to go to hospital when he caught something in his zip. It was in the middle of summer and the only long coat we had to cover it up was a white raincoat. It was hilarious what the lads was saying would happen when the nurse asked him what was wrong and he had to open his rain coat to show her. It is a good job it's not today; he would have to wait up to two to three hours.

But it healed up, and not to long after, he came to work, looking really worried. When asked what was wrong, he said he would have to get married, of course, with his luck his girlfriend was pregnant. We told him it is his own fault; he should have kept it zipped up. We urged him to change his name before the kid was born, can you imagine somebody, looking at the baby, saying he looks just like his dad, he's a Jinks.

My building days took me all over East London, to many large factories such as Bryant & Mays Matchmakers, an old workhouse, later turned into a factory, and now a luxurious block of apartments, called Manhattan Buildings. Then Clarnico's Sweet Factory down Carpenters Road, also Yardley's, where most of the girls worked packing cosmetics and perfumes, Conway Stewarts Pen Co., in Mile End opposite the then new Duke of Edinburgh's playing fields, where I watched Tony Carr (still with West Ham United) playing for East London Boys.

I carried out maintenance and rebuilding for 3 to 4 years at another firm, Oxos in Waterden road, Hackney Wick, (before Katie became the Oxo girl) and used to be invited to their Christmas parties. There I actually danced with Betty Wesley, one part of John and Betty Wesley the one time world amateur champions – she dances a lovely conga.

Another job I had was going around offices fixing modesty panels to the front of desks but I got a lot of complaints from the ladies whose modesty I was trying to protect. They complained that it was not worth buying and wearing Miniskirts if their legs were not going to be seen.

I was training with East Ham United football team at Savage Gardens, Beckton. The coach, Malcolm Allison, was the captain of West Ham at that time. Unfortunately, I left after having a row with another player whom I was also working with at Telefusion, Bethnal Green Road, opposite Pelicies Café. I should have stayed with East Ham; it was the one big chance that I had in football, but life goes on.

I was going out with a girl from the Isle of Dogs. Don't laugh at that name; she really was a nice girl and not a dog, although she did turn out to be rather a bitch. I discovered that she'd been two-timing me when I was in the army doing my National Service.

Whilst I was in the army mum got ill and had major surgery to remove one of her kidneys but, thank God, she did recover.

I came out of the army, and went back to the building trade. My young brother Terry died; apparently he fell over in the main road, hitting his head on the curb. His mate, Billy Gunn, who lived in the same street as us, Hedworth Street, picked him up and brought him home where he died.

I was working in Three Mill Lane at the time and as I walked along our street coming home from work, I sensed something was wrong. I was totally shattered when I was told of his death.

I will forever remember his funeral. As the cortege left Hedworth street it crossed into Rowsal street, up across Turners Road, under the railway bridge into Bede Road, around and across the Bow Common Lane, into Loxley Street with Chipperfields on the corner and on into Southern Grove past his school, where both sides of the road was crowded with kids.

It seemed the whole school had turned out, all the way up Southern Grove, to the Large Iron Gates at the entrance to the cemetery. The only noise I can remember, apart from some of our women crying, and some of the men, was the sound of the wheels of the hearse crunching the gravel as we slowly made our way up to the small church, and then out again, to finally lay my brother Terry to rest. Less than 20 years after, some heartless moron decided, to stop burials and turn the cemetery into a car park, a supermarket or a block of flats.

I was going through a rough time, everybody gets one. I was not in control and simply looked for a crutch to lean on. I had not been taught to think long term, but only how to spiv from day to day. Even now I still do not plan ahead.

At that time I turned to the church. I did not go searching for it, but came into a group of friends at a youth club and a whole new world appeared before me. Most of these friends were trainee nurses, doctors, and teachers, and all church goers. So I became a church goer and was surprised by how many good people I got to know and respect. It only lasted for approximately two years but I am glad of the experience.

The irresistible Bobbie Abbott, aged 18

Chapter 3

Bobbie Abbott: My first date

I must give the Methodist church in Bow Road a mention. For the short time I attended there with Maurise Wetherup, the priest always gave a good sermon and, as usual, the singing of the hymns and choruses were unequalled anywhere.

The youth club was excellent and I made many friends there. I introduced Maurise to Hackney Mashes Football. We were a man short in our team and I was sent to the gate of Hackney Marshes to get a ringer – somebody good to replace our missing player. There was Maurise, standing at the gate with his boots slung over his shoulders by the laces, still with his dog collar on.

The air was blue as usual when he entered the changing room and then there was complete silence when they saw his dog collar. What they did not know at the time was that Maurise had played semi-pro for Glentoran, the Belfast first division leaders at that time. To complete the story, I was awarded the two Wembley Cup Final tickets (issued to each club in them days) and took Maurise along to the famous twin towers to see Luton Town play Nottingham Forest. Maurise was a friend of Billy Bingham, the manager of Luton at that time, and *Abide With Me* was never sung better or louder.

I was playing football regularly and made a lot of friends. Weekends were fabulous; the Mile End Road was alive. All the pubs from Gardeners Corner (now Aldgate Circus) to Stratford, Maryland Point and still further, were crammed full with entertainment. Piano players, live bands, talent contests, they were all having a great time swinging away with the *Swinging Sixties,* from teddy boys to mods and rockers.

The mods turned up in their mohair suits from A. Whites, near to Stepney Green station, or Sauls in Hackney Road, driving their Scooters – Vespers, Lambrettas – most of them brought from Eddy Grinstead's in Burdett Road, near to the old Easton Hotel, at Limehouse. Eddy, who started up with a bike shop, then scooters, is now a multinational main car dealer. The Rockers were all there in their leathers and greasy hair, on their BSAs, and Triumphs.

The older lads, who were 20 to 30 year olds, mostly wore their Italian style suits and Perry Como raincoats. More and more of us in our 20s were buying our first cars; second-hand Wolseleys, Morris Oxfords, Austin Cambridges, Ford Zephyrs, Consuls, Vauxhall Veloxs, Victors and Humber's, to name a few. Most of these cars still had starting handles.

The first car I owned was a Jowett Javelin, a three forward and one reverse, three-stroke petrol engine, with running boards and black and white squares on the bonnet, doors and boot. I sold it for scrap iron to Philly Snooks, but I wish I'd kept it.

Once again I returned to work for Excelsior Biscuit Company in Thomas Road, Bow, and again Bobbie Abbott worked there. I still did not know her to talk to and when I left my sister Doreen, who also worked there, got friendly with Bobbie, and arranged a date for us. Two weeks earlier Pete Murray, a famous DJ, film star and TV personality whom I'd met whilst playing football for Strollers United (a Camden based team, run by my brother-in-law Bobby Appleby's brother, Alf) had given me two tickets for a recording of the *Six-Five-Special* at the two I's club near Carnaby Street, W1.

There I was, all dressed up for our first date, excited and nervous, knocking on the door of number 8 Knapp Road. I had waited 22 years for a date like this and she kept me waiting at the door for about ten minutes, but the wait was well worth it. At first sight, you'd noticed her beautiful reddish, auburn hair, very white skin, funny cute nose, and sparkling eyes, a challenging all-round (in the right places) appearance. Of course I'd noticed her for years.

I'd stood on our corner (the large pavement area outside the funeral parlour at the junction of Campbell Road and Devons Road) where all the lads used to congregate, and watched her come and go from her house at 8 Knapp Road. She was always a very popular girl with plenty of friends who seemed always to be knocking on her door. It seemed to be their meeting place and they would sit on the window ledge and wall outside her house, listening to her records. Every boy in Bow must have fancied her but, like me, never had the nerve to chat her up.

I remember Bobbie way back when the girls wore bobbie sox, black pedal pushers and white tops, or velvet collared, teddy boy (Edwardian) dog toothed jackets. It seemed to be a uniform and we would stand on that corner for hours, watching all the girls go by.

You will remember I went to school next door to her house and, for a number of years, delivered coke to her mum. I worked at the Excelsior Biscuits, and then we'd worked at Bell Moors sweet company at Solway Street, Bow, E3. Solly, the owner, employed approximately 45 staff and I was being trained as a sugar boiler, or sweet maker, making toffee butter brazils.

I did not work there for long but saw her daily and she looked sweeter than anything I made. I even went on the firm's beano down to Southend – where else? It was a funny coincidence but if fate was trying to get us together, it did not work out that day. Bobbie and her mate Maureen Carr (daughter of Tiny Carr, the famous TV wrestling referee) found their own way home. I was about 17 at that time, a slow starter, but knew the difference between girls and boys.

With the girls they want their men dressed up like Prince Charming, but with boys it's the opposite, they don't like girls wearing any clothes at all!

Anyhow, back to our first date. Bobbie asked to see the tickets, and found to my embarrassment that they were out of date.

What a start. There I was on a dream of a date, and I'd messed up. I said I would arrange it for another time, and asked if she would like to see a film instead. *Oklahoma*, the musical, was on at the Rex in Stratford.

'I'd love to,' she said, and off we went down the end of Knapp Road to the Junction of Campbell Road and Devons Road, past Baileys, the pet food shop, and Cooks, the bike shop, and waited for the 86A from Limehouse.

We hopped on the bus – life had a new meaning – it was seven stops to the Rex at Stratford. Up Campbell Road to Bow Road, past Ronnie and Reggie Kray's club, past the Popular Civic Theatre, Bow Church and the Regal Cinema, over the old iron bridge (before the flyover, with or without Ginger Marks buried inside) was thought of. Bow locks (don't read that too fast) straight on through to Stratford, passing Yardley's, the Cosmetics firm on the left, before stopping outside Cooks Pie and Eel Shop, opposite the Rex. I got the tickets and in we went.

It seemed Bobbie did not know the rules. Maybe nobody had told her, or maybe it was that mix-up with the films, and if it had been *Oklahoma* instead of *Birth of a Baby*, things would have been different. Indeed, I would not have had my face slapped (I told you she was a challenge).

Our first date nearly became our last; she said she was not that sort of girl. I explained that it was her beauty and the excitement of being near to her that had brought out the beast in me. It took me a long time before I was ready for singing *Oh, What a Beautiful Morning*.

I really did want to see that film, *Oklahoma*. There we were in the back row – she did understand that we only sat back there because I was long sighted.

The Rex in Stratford, E14, was a grand old cinema. I say old because I'm sure I was getting electric shocks every time I got near to her, and she laughingly apologised when her cigarette burnt my hand that had wandered, with a mind of its own, to within six inches of her thigh.

And then that film came on just as Bobbie was returning from the Ladies room. Ha, here she comes. I'd been sitting there nursing my hand, planning my next move. She sat down, I had already left my hand on the back of her chair – smart move that – and then the film started.

Bobbie mumbled something like 'I hope you did not plan this. This isn't the film you said was showing,' and reached for her cigarette. I promptly withdraw my arm from the back of her seat.

'Do you get anything right?' she said.

'I'm working on it,' I replied and apologised again. I asked her if she wanted to watch the film and she said 'No, let's go.' I could not get out of there quickly enough.

I don't think Bobbie had expected this on our first date. I'd been out with a few girls, one at a time, and got quite serious with one, before getting called up to do national service.

There I was at Winchester with the Royal Green Jackets – that was the riffle brigade, Kings Royal Riffles – and the Oxfordshire and Buckinghamshire Light Infantry amalgamated. I was never a private, but a hundred and seventy steps a minute rifleman, and that's not at the double.

Winchester Barracks, 1957

I could march faster than most people can run, but being a rifleman should mean I had perfect eyesight. Alas, my right eye is lazy and I can only see a blur, and they did not cater for left-handed riffles – not in the Green Jackets.

Because you could not do the correct riffle drill with a left-handed Lea Enfield, you could not march at the trail – that is marching with the riffle at your side, parallel with the ground and not on your shoulder – and when I took sight with my left eye, being a right handed riffle, as you pulled the bolt back, the bolt usually clouted you in the mouth.

But obeying orders I persevered and became a marksman, as did nearly everybody. The sergeant was barking out orders (even the bullets did as they were told) and of course, I was good at basic training.

For some reason I was put into the end part of the barracks, which was an L shaped room that kept our four beds separate from the others. The other three privates in there with me were university graduates, two from Oxford and one from Cambridge. The Cambridge one was Peter De Llisle who played cricket for Middlesex.

His father owned a tea plantation in Ceylon, long before the days of the teabag. The next one from Oxford was Viscount Evans, no relation to Chris Evans, or Godfrey Evans of course. Chris was not even born then, but Godfrey was already a legend.

The third one, from Oxford, remembered only as Adrian, might has been related to Adrian Mole. A smashing bloke, but could not march and salute without coming out of the salute with his left foot and left arm going forward at the same time. It was hilarious and I swear even the Sergeant smiled.

The more Adrian practised it, the worst he got. But he must have got it right in the end because the next time I saw him was when he was inspecting the guard of which I was one – I did not volunteer – they had made him an officer. And true to form, he put me on a charge for having dirty brasses after spending twelve weeks training and living together in the same room. The next time I saw him was in Wales (overseas posting) in a place called Sennibridge near to the Brecon Beacon. Don't ask me what we were doing there because nobody knew.

Then one day a load of Territorial Army sorts arrived along with my old officer mate, Adrian.

He and the TA would go off for a few hours a day, then when they got back it was party time. It was a wonderful summer that year, and yours truly, with another squaddie (Alfie Clutterbuck) decided to go paddling, which you would think was quite harmless.

The river was bloody freezing. It was like putting your feet in a fridge and that's exactly what somebody else had thought; they were using the river to cool down there best champagne and wine. So we thought we would sample it, and had nearly finished the second bottle before Adrian appeared on the scene.

Lucky for me it was him, because any other officer would have automatically put us on a charge.

Terry: rest in peace

Chapter 4

Shocks to the system

Back to Winchester, next door to the Assizes where they have the famous round table, you know, King Arthur and all his knights. Then back to Civvy Street and back to Hedworth Street, the year 1960. Back home to the place where you are treated the best, and grumble the most.

Home with my family, and Mum's bread pudding and all's right with the world. No, it does not work like that.

First my girl friend of over three years decided that my armour had lost some of its shine and whilst I was away fighting for my Country – well drinking champers in Wales – she found herself another knight and told me to get on my horse. At the same time my brother Terry died.

I was in a complete daze for weeks, even months, but I gradually came out of it and decided that life goes on.

I even left the building trade and went to work at Charringtons brewery and got friendly with a work mate, Ray Rimmel. One day he said to me, 'I has had enough of this Dan, how about coming into business with me?'

'What as?' said I.

'Well, you seem to know everything; you have worked everywhere.'

'I suppose we'll need some cash up front, won't we?'

'Every business needs some outlay,' he said.

'No, it don't,' I said. 'With window cleaning you don't need a penny. All you need is a scrim, and a bucket and ladder.'

And that's exactly what we did.

It started off slowly and then blossomed. It grew quickly and Ray wanted to add office cleaning, expand and become a limited company.

We were becoming too big too quickly and I also discovered that we had a mutual friend. Ray's best friend was only the guy that I had been kicked into touch for whilst doing my National service. This caused quite a lot of trouble as I feel Ray used it to annoy me, resulting in me turning my back on what was, and still is, quite a large company, which was, of course, my idea.

Me at Southend Pier,1960

So there I was in 1960, walking along the Mile End Road where I meet a friend called Alfie Bunyon, We went into the Terminus café, near to the corner of Grove Road and Mile End Road. The Terminus café was a meeting place for groups of young and not so young students, along with would-be-actors.

My elder brother, Patsy, was in there with his Toymbee Hall lot, usually discussing how they would have improved on Richard the Third with their new style of method acting. I remember one day they were asked to leave.

When asked what one of them was doing laying prostate on a table at the end of the café, they replied that he was imagining he was a needle in a haystack. This apparently had something to do with their method acting, which gave the owner of the café the proverbial needle. He asked them to leave and find themselves another haystack.

Anyhow, in the café that day, Alf introduced me to a group at one of the tables, and a whole new world opened up. The conversations were certainly different to what I was used to – they were talking about the church, God, the universe and what's at the end of space, minus more space.

I sat there listening, not saying anything, and then a ginger Irishman was asking me my opinion.

Welcome to the world of Christianity, or in this case, Maurise Weatherup, whom I had not noticed till then had a dog collar around his neck.

Now I did not really have an opinion, but I heard someone offering to answer what God's reason was for my young brother Terry dying at 14 years of age and in his last week at school.

'Come along to church on Sunday and I will try to give you an answer,' he replied, and I was in.

I was not like that guy the atheist, the wealthy man who set out to prove Christianity wrong and finished up a Christian himself and went on to write the book, *Who moved the stone?*

I still find myself, when I am with my inner thoughts, wondering if I ever believed in God. But I am sure that for nearly a couple of years I found happiness and contentment. Like the time we went from door to door delivering 'Feed the Mind' envelopes, and the fantastic response we got when collecting the envelopes. There really are a lot of good hearted, generous people out there – and I don't mean the rich, buying their way to heaven.

And later, how I got completely taken in with the singing of hymns and the choruses when we went to Central Hall, opposite the Houses of Parliament.

We went away soon after at Easter time to Cliff College in Matlock, Derbyshire. It reminded me of that wonderful University town of Heidelberg in Germany where they made the film, *The Student Prince.*

There was dozens of different denominations and all kinds of religions, all helping with large tents, the cooking, and laying and clearing the tables. People would get up and share how they had found God. That weekend left me being a different person.

Not long afterwards the group of friends that I had become so attached to seemed to break up. Some went back to university while others became teachers, doctors, and nurses.

I returned to the building trade, and only saw Maurise when we played football together. My visits to the Methodist church in Bow Road just seemed to stop.

So, back to Bobbie. She seemed so sure of herself and so confident, I thought she was quite posh. She'd come from a good family and her Mum always used to tip me well when I delivered the coke.

She always seemed to have new clothes on, and this being way back in the 1950/60s, when a woman said she had nothing to wear, it meant exactly that. These were the days when the girls would nip up to Crisp Street market or up the Roman on a Saturday morning to buy a yard of material, in order to make a skirt to go out in on the same night. By the end of the 1960s, they were wearing ⅛th of a yard miniskirts.

We started dating two or three time a week, and after a few mouths her hair needed washing less frequently. By this time, I had become two different people.

First, there was this insecure, mild mannered, shy, church going lad of 21 and second there was a foul mouthed, hard working lout, playing the foreman on the building site.

Of course nobody away from work knew that side of me. Even my family called me the *Preacher* as, unlike most of them, I never used bad language in the house and certainly not in the presence of Bobbie.

By 1961 an inseparable love had blossomed between us and I could not envisage life without her.

She still asks me if I get anything right, and I still reply, 'I'm working on it'. But up until now, after 40 years of married life, I still have not changed.

Bobbie's mum, Margaret, died after we'd been courting for about a year, apparently from a broken heart. She had no illness but lost the will to live after the sudden death of her beloved Tom, (Bobbie's dad had died 4 years earlier). Bobbie and I got married about a year after, in 1961.

We got married in All Hallows Church in Devon's Road, Bow, E3, and had the reception in the local pub, called The Bun House. The story behind the name is that many years ago the owner, a widow, had an only son who went to sea and never returned. Each year at Easter time the widow put a light in the window and hung up a hot cross bun, which was the son's favourite, there in the window waiting for him to return. Each new owner of the pub carries on this tradition. The pub is in Devon's Road, near the junction of Campbell and Knapp Road.

As Bobbie had been born and lived in 8 Knapp Road all her life, she took over the rent book and continued to live there with her married sister

Joan her husband and their children all living upstairs, and Bobbie living downstairs. So, once married, we did not have the trouble of searching for somewhere to live. After three years her sister needed a larger place to live and moved across the road to number 1 Knapp Road.

It was a good place to live and we were quite happy there. Bobbie knew all the neighbours, having lived there for 20 years, and we were only 50 yards from the junction of Devon's Road, Campbell Road and Violet Road. There were three newsagents, a butcher's, baker's, post office, two betting shops, two greengrocers, a flower shop, shoe shop, dress shop and even a funeral parlour.

Less than five minutes from our house, Crisp Street Market stretched from Sprats Pet Food factory in Morris Road all the way up to East India Dock Road – although you had to go over Stink-house Bridge to get there – up Devon's Road, past the Widow's Son, to St Andrews Hospital. Under the bridge there used to be Stony Hills, a mountain of sand-shingle with one old tree trunk growing out of the top to which we had naturally attached a rope to make a swing. I'd bet there wasn't a kid in Bow, or the surrounding areas, who had not swung on that tree.

On that very junction of Campbell Road / Devon's Road was a funeral parlour and, at that time, a very large pavement area.

Since I arrived in Bow, this was always our meeting place. I suppose just like today there would be a group of young boys and girls larking about, making a noise. The names have changed; we had names like, Ronny Clarke, David Cohen, Johnny King, Jimmy Horncastle, Brian Wood, Brian Hood, David Valentine, Harry Abraham's, Mickey Calvey, Alfie Cole, Jimmy Stubbs, Terry Farmer, Roy Allison, David Benmor. I suppose now the names would be Ali, Mohammed, Luke, Slim and Rory. Still just kids larking about though, and making a noise.

At the top Campbell Road, was Bow Road. There used to be a dance hall called Bow Palace and a few doors along was The Double R Club. As I grew older the Krays got better known; when I was 20 they were 25.

The Krays were everywhere, and everybody knew them. Lucky enough, they never, so I believe, got into the sporting world, although we could do with them down at White Hart Lane to get rid of the chap on loan from Arsenal.

If you went down Devon's Road, towards Bow Common Lane you passed Fern Street. For as long back as I remember, and longer according to Bobbie's oldest neighbours, there was a local group of people, called the

Fern Street Settlement, who had for years collected items such as, toys, books and bits and pieces, and put them into bundles. They had a small arch, and any kid who could walk through would get a farthing bundle.

Further down Devon's Road, on the left hand side, there stood a small building, all on its own. The rest of the shops and houses had been blown up during the war and this is where I spent many nights after school, making darts and dartboards for Dicky Hood. Just past there, on the corner of Bow Common Lane, was a bombed out church, directly opposite the Nag's Head pub. This church became our camp when we were schoolboys; we would, clamber around inside, light fires. We were always in there, so I suppose I can claim I always went to church when I was young.

Anyhow, Bobbie and I settled down to married life; I was still in the building trade and worked at Gamages in Holborn as a painter, which was quite interesting. Every Christmas time they had a grotto in a large room and the kids could ride round in a large model train. Months before, we would have to repaint the room with grotto scenery and animals.

This was the first time I'd really worked for a long period in central London and I quite liked the buzz, and the excitement. Bobbie was working for Charlotte Hilton along with her two sisters, Ena and Ruby. Bobbie was a cutter and finisher, Ena was lacing and designing, while Ruby was a sample machinist.

The firm made lingerie for private and large department stores, and top named shops including Harrods. Some of the garments were named Roberta and Deborah and, as Ena designed them, she could name them after her family and friends.

Their boss, Mrs B, being Jewish and from Germany, supplied the correct undergarments to the Secret Service for some of the women spy's that was operating in France during the war.

We got quite friendly with an old schoolmate of mine, David Washborne and his wife Maureen. David was a good singer and weekends we would pub crawl; The White Horse on Burdett Road, The Aberdeen at the corner of Roman Road and Grove Road, and many others in and around the area. With Dave getting up to sing, we would get free drinks from the landlord.

Bobbie joined the Royal Charlie's pub darts team. It was owned by a well-known character named Buck Ryan, who also ran a betting shop in Devon's Road.

The Charlie's was in Crisp Street and it was always buzzing with excitement. Me and my old mate Davey Washborne built Buck a stage, and every weekend and darts nights, Buck would hire a piano player. All the local talent, led by Dave, would get up and give a song and do their party piece.

Then at the end of the night, Buck Ryan, would put a tea-towel round the back of his neck, shove a cap on his head, pick up a shotgun, and sing The legionnaire's song, *Good Bye, Good Bye, I wish you all the luck, Good Bye,* and we'd all get in a line behind him and, waving our handkerchiefs, would march and sing-a-long to the door. One night when we would not go home after singing the song half-a-dozen times, Buck fired the shotgun and shattered the dartboard, then threatened us with the shotgun just to get rid of us.

We all ran out, jumped in our Consuls and Zephyrs, and went home to our council flats. They certainly were happy days. I was back in the building trade again and it was a lovely summer's day.

The ground was rock hard; we were digging foundations for a new boiler house at Bow-locks. That same morning, in the local paper, there was a few columns about Bow pottery which, we discovered, was quite famous and also very rare.

There was Stan the man, always ready for a laugh, and big Ron, a smashing bloke but a bit slow on the uptake, digging the trench that I had marked out.

Big Ron stood back after loosening up the earth with the pickaxe. Stan the man stepped forward with his shovel and started to shovel out the dirt. For a laugh, he threw it over my foot, so I stooped down and picked up this old clay pipe.

'Look what I've found Stan.'

It was all dirty, the cup end, where you put the tobacco in, was in the shape of an Indian Chief's head, and it had a 3-inch stem.

'Whatever you get on that,' said Stan, 'I want half, because I shovelled it out of the hole, I bet it's old Bow pottery.'

Big Ron pushed forward, 'Make that three ways. I dug it up in the first place, so I want my share.'

After some argument, and a little bit of encouragement by Stan and myself, we decided to sell our shares to Big Ron, who was convinced he had a genuine antique. He placed it to one side and threatened to chop off anybody's hands if they got near it.

Stan went for a leak, and soon after different people came past, wanting to marvel at Big Ron's prize possession. Even I thought that I'd done a wrong 'un until Big Ron started to throw the pickaxe wildly into the ground like a madman, He had come across thousands of these clay pipes and it became obvious to him that he had been well and truly had.

He came towards Stan and me, with his pickaxe held above his head, demanding his money back. Lucky for us though, he saw the funny side of it.

I kept that clay-pipe for years on the mantelpiece where friends could see it and Bobbie always says 'Please don't ask him where he got that pipe.' But of course they always do and I've spent many a happy hour reliving my time in the building trade. I've sold the pipe three times to date.

I had not seen Big Ron for years, and was happy for him when I heard he'd dug up an old treasure. He married a rich widow and moved to America, where he probably lives on an Indian reservation.

The use of street signs to identify buildings goes back to a decision of the Corporation of London in 1580 which ordered that "shopkeepers shall hang out signs at their shops"

Chapter 5

Enter the Eagle

After seven years of marriage, the year was 1968 (England had not yet got forgotten they had won the world cup).

The building trade was going through a tough time and I had taken a driving job for office furniture firm called S.O.S. (Southwark Office Supplies) delivering office furniture to banks and offices in the city. I got talking to some of the messengers and discovered that most of them were home owners, having brought their homes through their banks at a reduced interest rate. I thought to myself, I'll have some of that, and promptly applied.

In the square mile (the city), before they built the Nat West Tower or the Lloyds Oil Refinery, city gents would walk around in top hats and with umbrellas, messengers in claw hammer jackets with different colours for different banks, and the guys from the stock exchange with brightly coloured striped suits and shirts.

There were thousands of messenger delivery boys and, with so many people coming and going, the city was alive.

The fish market caused chaos, and the through road from the Tower of London past Billingsgate, Upper Thames Street into lower Thames Street and on to Blackfriars, was hell. And to add to that, up until 1966 we still had smog. Everyone walked about with smog masks on. Thank God for the Clean Air Act – the best law ever passed before or since.

I had applied to Lloyds Bank and Barclays Bank for a messenger's job, I had interviews with both banks and was offered both jobs, but decided two jobs would be too much. I accepted Barclays offer, hence the Eagle chapter title, and started work for them in 1967 with my pay being £11.80 per week (or £11 16 shillings in old money).

We were paid cash each week in 10/- notes. I think they gave us it all in ten-bob notes (the old word for shilling is bob) to make it seem more.

At around the same time as starting work with the bank, we had notice to quit No 8 Knapp Road, and were offered a number of choices where to live. We choose Belfron Towers, overlooking the North entrance of the Blackwall tunnel – in fact, overlooking almost everywhere. Our street door was on the fifteenth floor but we lived on the sixteenth floor – stay with me, concentrate – the next door neighbour on the right lived on the fourteenth floor and, of course, the left side neighbours lived on the fifteenth floor.

We were so high up the next door neighbours (nice people) used to excrete on the pigeons below. One day we looked out of the window and thought that there was a fire below. It looked like smoke, but we found out it was snowing below us.

All our post was marked *air mail*, and of course we became members of the mile high club, although Bobbie will claim she never joined, or signed up for any club. Deborah was born on the 19th December 1968.

Getting our feet back on the ground, I returned to the Eagle (Barclays Bank). These were the dark days without technology, when the clearing of cheques was done by hand, from all over the country, and when you had to wait up to three whole days just to get a cheque cleared. To get a special clearance, it could take you all of 2 or 3 hours, and to get a loan you could talk to a manager.

These were the days when painters wore white and even used brushes, when you could get change from a bus conductor, a good morning from the milkman if you gave his horse an apple and the days at Barclays, when you were not allowed, if you were a messenger, to play sport with the clerical staff. When the dining hall had an imaginary line down the middle, keeping clerical and messengers apart, and when Saturday morning was part of your working week if you were a messenger but overtime if you were clerical.

If you think I'm moaning, you're wrong, I believe this is, and should be, the way of life – if you can't stand the heat, get out of the kitchen.

This is what I did (well, not exactly). I got a move up to the kitchen, or servery. I believe in bettering yourself and the fact that I got paid more money had nothing to do with my move.

Although it was a very servile job, I learnt a lot in the servery. Firstly I learnt about preparing and laying tables for whatever meal or occasion there was; it became second nature. I was taught about oysters – how to open, clean and turn them, and lobster – how to break and prepare them.

I got acquainted with quail's eggs, crabs, (one of my best friends was a crab), game and grouse. We served salmon, Dover sole, trout, smoked eels, and turbot. I was actually trained as a kind of house butler; I cleaned silver, polished plates, glasses, genuine James Second Silver Crown Derby, decanted port and daily prepared the best wines, clarets, and champagnes.

Our daily job was to prepare for the amount of persons attending, always expecting a few extra latecomers. The Directors numbered 60 plus.

Two or three times a month we had evening dinners parties with V.I.P. visitors including prime ministers Margaret Thatcher, Ted Heath and Harold Wilson, cabinet ministers by the score, (although not all at once), Archbishops, Lords, Ladies, envoys from abroad, royalty from home and abroad – one young Lady of about 75, the Queen Mum, came and insisted in meeting our cook and saying a few kind words of thanks to us for our good food and service.

Twice a month I would go to the Chairman, Sir Anthony Tuke's house to arrange, prepare and serve dinner for up to ten people. The chairman and his family lived in Frognall, Hampstead, just up the road from Camden Town.

I often thought that if Mum could see me now, serving food and drink to some very famous and rich friends of the Tuke's, she'd be proud of me.

We catered for all seasons. Grouse on the twelfth of August, at the Lord Mayor of the City Of London's annual dinner in November, (with a saucer of milk under the table for his cat).

The Christmas lunches with turkey, goose, walnuts, Christmas pudding with brandy butter, brandy cream and brandy to pour on the mince pies, having first removed the lid of the pie. We had special names for the directors, such as 'Napper' Wilde. He was called that because he had the habit of slapping the back of his head with the flat of his hand, and was also instrumental in introducing the Barclaycard to the UK. I should slap him on the head.

Then there was the 'Pirate from Penzance', a likeable chap who liked to read the newspapers laid out for guests (he always walked off with one tucked under his arm). Then there was also 'Wingy' (chairman, Mr Tuke), an ex-prisoner of war who served in the RAF. He was a remarkable man who walked with his arms stretched sideways. There were many others with a special mention of Lord Carrington who, when one of our team (Les Dixon) said to him, 'Good morning, sir. I saw your bridge where you won your medal at the weekend.' (Dixon had been to France; he was interested in World Wars). Lord Carrington answered, 'Not quite correct, Dixon. The men who won it, they died there. I received it for them.'

The opening of The New Drury Lane Theatre, in 1976 was quite a night and along we went – a team of eight from Barclays, to serve the drinks and sandwiches. With the Royal Marines for security, The Duke and Duchess of Kent arrived.

There were also film stars and famous actors and actresses. It was interesting, mingling with stars like Sir Alex Guinness, Sir John Mills, and Kenneth Moore to name a few. And to think my old grandmother used to sell flowers just outside.

Then there was the Debutantes Coming Out Ball, near to the Albert Hall. A magnificent building, and along came all these Hooray 'Enerys with their Debs, dancing to a live band, and us pouring bucks fizz down their throats. We could not open the champagne quick enough. The inside of my thumb and first finger was scratched and bleeding after opening the bottles. How the other 2% can live it up!

The American bicentennial party at Greenwich was somewhat different, but I did manage to acquire a special bottle of champagne. It was given to me by one of the guests and is long gone now – only the cork remains. Looking back, I did see life working for Barclays.

We served drinks and bites at the head office when Barclays sponsored the Everest expedition, and I got to meet and talk to Chris Bonnington, I never did go up on a mountain though, but later on I did claim my personal mountain, or rather run my Marathon. Aged 46 I entered a half-marathon and trained around the streets of South Woodford.

It was a late frosty, foggy, dark November evening as I glided down George Lane (still running like a young Gisele) past the new Sainsbury's, where they pulled down that lovely church (note I was going downhill) to the roundabout between two cars and whoosh, I hadn't seen it, a tow rope.

The Jag in front kept going whilst the Jag behind braked hard. Two Jags? No, it couldn't be – he only had a bike then although it could've been him trying to save petrol). The back fender came off, over I went and I lay on the curb with the tow car stopping, close to my arm. Both drivers got out, and one called me a silly old B------- (I did not like the 'old' bit) while the other mentioned something to do with Claybury, a local hospital well known for accommodating slightly deranged people, which of course he thought I was – there are some who would agree with him! After cooling down, they asked me if I was all right.

I said I was, having counted my arms and legs. So they tied their cars together, and away they went. There I was, sitting in the gutter in shorts and a vest, apparently now in shock. My legs, ribs and head was grazed, I was freezing cold because I'd stopped running and there was nobody about. I had no money in my pocket to make a phone call (I had no pockets) and I shouldn't have got up to walk home – I was a couple of miles away – but I got home somehow, can't remember how though, and I might have climbed a mountain on the way home.

I continued working in the directors' servery until 1978 or 79, during which time my mother died. I did not know at that time the disastrous effect her death would have on myself and the breaking up of my family.

I will not dwell on this subject for long except suffice to say whatever reasons exist, none should be unforgivable.

I remember soon after her death standing in the plush green room, an ante-room outside the main servery and dining room. The walls were furnished with large mirrors and expensive paintings, by Sir Alfred Munnings and other prominent painters including Field Marshal Mountbatten, and thinking how unfair life is, my old mum had never seen anything like this room in her whole life.

It was light years from the room in Plender Street, Camden Town, where my dad had broken windows from the outside, grabbed handfuls of soot from up the chimney and thrown it around the room to enable him to get a payment for bomb damage or bomb blast.

Looking around the room you noticed the Munnings paintings; his famous country scene depicting the farmer in the field and a passer by telling him that war had broke out, and the marvellous horses he painted. Immediately it brought back memories of Derby days, when the old man and Uncle Bill borrowed a horse and cart and sent me round to all the fruit and veg stalls to get wooden boxes. We collected hundreds, and loaded them on the cart and tied them on. Early on Wednesday, Derby Day morning, we made our way down to Epson Downs.

The boxes were soon sold, some twice, as I borrowed them back, and resold them.

The posh punters would use them to stand on to see the races, and afterwards to sit on around the picnic blanket. We would gather them up afterwards and take them home, for firewood.

I had by this time moved from Belfron Towers, Poplar, E14, and brought my first house in Ilford (before the floods) for £3,500. My mortgage was £28 per calendar month including mortgage protection.

I then sold that house and moved to 83 Hayes Drive, South Hornchurch, with a staggering mortgage of £5,800 in 1970. My mortgage had now gone up to £38 per month including mortgage protection.

I had been with the bank about ten years and was approaching that funny age 40, so I decided to leave the bank and go into a cleaning company set up by my brother Brian.

On my leaving day in November 1979 I was advised against leaving at that time by one of the Directors of the bank, Mr M. Buxton (a former Rowing Blue for Cambridge University). He brought back memories of my childhood days when, weeks prior to the university boat race day, my uncle Bill would get us making thousands of miniature oars out of potatoes caskets (from Jersey).

Those caskets were made from bamboo; we got them from the greengrocer. We would break them down and cut the bamboo into 3 inch lengths, shape each one into a miniature oar and dip both ends into either a light or dark blue paint.

Once dried, we crossed two of them together and tied a blue bow around the middle with a pin at the back. My uncle and me would take them down to Putney, by the river Thames, and sell them on the day of the boat race to the thousands of university supporters lining the bridges on both banks of the Thames.

Mum and us kids would work long hours getting them made and the rewards were not worth all the hard work. We were never paid but I will always remember the good times I enjoyed at the bank, and there were quite a few.

They were a great bunch to work with at Barclays, quick witted and funny. I arrived late one morning, made my excuses – that the starter motor on my car had fallen off. The next morning Jimmy Jenkins was late coming in on his bike. In he came and shouted out, 'Sorry I'm late, you won't believe this, but I was cycling down the road and ran into a starter motor, causing me to crash!'

I tell you we had more excuses than British Rail and we always had an excuse to visit Leadenhall Street Market with its glass roof. The market, off Gracechurch Street, was built especially to serve the city's canteens, serveries and thousands of small kitchens, in the banks, insurance companies, and the Stock Exchange. It was, and still is, a busy place where you can buy fresh fish, cheese, fruit and vegetables. Most mornings there are queues, buying and ordering for their daily lunches.

The many cafés and tea rooms were also a meeting place for messengers to sort out and exchange documents, credits, post and cheques, and of course it had a few pubs which always seemed full – the city being a very dusty place.

But I was 40 years old and needed a change, so I left the bank and went into a cleaning company, self-employed with my brothers, Brian and Joe.

The cleaning company was quite a success; there were lots of clubs and offices in the West End, and among the clubs we cleaned was the Embassy Club in New Bond Street. Day and night, it was always busy; I can still remember Elaine Stretch doing Cinderella twice daily as a Christmas panto.

We would rush in after every performance to clean up. There were dance groups, photographers, and models and at night it was the place to be seen. Royalty, film stars, sportsmen – anybody who was anybody would turn up and we would have to get it ready for the late night (very early morning) Champagne Breakfast in the lovely setting of an Agatha Christie book, made especially for the occasion.

As well as the Embassy club, we contracted for the Heaven Club which was in Charring Cross, underneath the very arches made famous by Flanagan and Allen. Also we would clean up after the Berkeley Square Ball, where each year they would actually raffle a Rolls Royce, drink champagne till it came out of their ears, and have the time of their lives. Rich people can really let their hair down – they know how to live – but alas I never did hear a nightingale sing in Berkeley Square (or did I ever dream that I would actually live nearby).

Another club I cleaned and looked after was the Director's Lodge in St James, managed by a chap called Richard Odorse who was also the doorman and bouncer. He could be a perfect gentleman one minute and an animal the next – a two Dan Cararty man.

He had a silver disc plaque signed and given to him by Francis Albert, or Frank Sinatra as we know him, after acting as his bodyguard when Sinatra came over to the United Kingdom on tour.

Richard also ran the snooker hall in Leicester Square. It used to be a famous dance hall right next door to the Warner Bros. Picture House where, whilst queuing, you were always entertained by the street artists doing their acts; sand dancers, singers and escape artists to name a few.

I find there's still a buzz there, but nowadays I'm glad to get away. When I was in my teens it had a kind of glamour to it, just walking around, down Tin Pan Alley, Friday Mills, Humphrey Little's Jazz Club, The two Is, Carnaby Street, Ronny Scott's, the Dominion, Paramount and Talk of The Town. I could go on all day about London. I actually feel sorry for people who were not born here in London.

The cleaning company was going great until The Embassy Club was sold. We arrived one morning and the locks had been changed so we could not get in. I then decided to do something different. My brothers, Brian, Patsy and Joey, had opened a greengrocer's shop in South Woodford and was ready to move on to something bigger. So I made them an offer for the fruit and veg business and brought them out. Bobbie and Debbie and I moved into the shop in Darby Road, South Woodford which at that time, in early 1979, was a good place to live.

It had a good community, smashing people and a mixed race of customers – we seemed to fit in nicely, Debbie went to the local school, Churchfields, I got to know what the customers wanted and was soon supplying to local pubs, restaurants, clubs and schools.

South Woodford seemed like a village, surrounded by Main Road, to Epping Forest, Buckhurst Hill, Chigwell, North Circular Road. Near enough to the city and the West End, and within easy reach of the five London Airports. It was good enough for Winston Churchill's old constituency. His statue stands at the top of South Woodford High Road just opposite The Churchill Club, named after him, and near to the Cricketers pub, which became our local.

Quite often horses or cattle would get out of their grazing fields and go wandering up and down the local roads, I think the farmer let them out on purpose following his row (going back years) concerning cattle food. It seems that the local council found out that the farmer used to cut all the grass up and down South Woodford and along Snaresbrooks to feed his cattle, and in their usual wisdom they decided to charge him for it.

He said, 'No thanks, cut the grass yourselves, and (do the unthinkable with it).' Of course the poor council could not find anybody to cut it for nothing. There's got to be a moral somewhere in this story.

Anyhow, not letting the grass grow under my feet, I'll make hay and move on, I used to go to Spitalfields early every morning buying the fruit and veg from the wholesalers, and because of the different nationalities using my shop, I was buying goods for Chinese, Asian, Indian, and other countries. Items I'd never heard of, and certainly could not spell. Of course, word got around that if you ran out of anything night or day, Danny would get it for you.

Dozens of times I was knocked up late at night, sometimes even when I was in bed asleep. Down I would go, and open the cold pot up to keep the customers happy, I used to spell avocado as advocado and people would let me know, so daily I gave them a little spelling mistake and they would get at me about it, something they could not do at the new Sainsbury's which opened up soon after us buying the shop.

The fact that Sainsbury's got permission, a) from the Council, and b) from the Church leaders, to pull down a lovely old church and play school – a clubhouse for guides – just to build a store, had nothing to do with my clients not shopping there. But their feelings soon changed. They forgot the old church and business drifted away from me.

To be fair, it did give work to a lot of people, I think the Vicar finished up on the bacon counter. Things got tough, Bobbie was working in the shop, and Debbie changed schools; from Churchfields to Woodbridge High School.

They had made a lot of friends in Woodford and enjoyed living in the area. I had settled into the community and even met a mate who was scouting for Watford. He asked me if I would consider becoming a scout and invited me up to Watford.

I did not ask to go there, I'm just full of football (some would say that's not all I'm full of) but away I went for tea and biscuits at Vicarage Road. I was taken into a room and introduced to Graham Taylor, Bertie Mee, and Tom Whally.

There were handshakes all round, and a few words from Graham who had to rush off. I was a bit annoyed Elton John was not there, but you can't have everything.

I was invited to join the scouting team and told I could claim expenses, was given a club badge and that was that.

Talking to Bertie Mee, I could understand how he won the double; his knowledge of football is to be admired. At that time he knew (I think) the name of nearly every up and coming youngster in the UK. I'll always remember him telling me what especially to look for; a natural left footed, left sided, redhead. Size don't matter, full back, fleet of foot, must be able to tackle (that's where the red head comes in). Apparently it was then and still is the hardest position to fill. Watford was, and still is, a great family club.

Good people, and with Graham Taylor in charge again, quite a good team. Incidentally, I've always supported Spurs, and was glad to see George Graham go, so we can return to flair football.

Back to Woodford and my shop, Sainsbury's was winning my customers, and business was up and down. The winter of 1982/83 was practically bad.

I'll never forget one night it was very cold, and when we went to bed it was snowing hard outside. The gullies on the roof were packed with snow and it turned to ice. Fresh snow started to fall, melted on top of the ice and came in under the tiles, leaking into the bedrooms and all the way through the building (three floors) to the shop on the ground floor.

We had buckets, pots and pans in every room, tipping them in the bath every time they got full up.

At about 2am I decided to get out on the roof and clear the gullies of ice. It was freezing cold and snowing hard but I managed to get them clear. Of course by this time it was 3 am and I had to go to the market, at Stratford.

Wet and cold I climbed into my large diesel van, but the pipe from the tank to the engine had frozen, I got a piece of rag, soaked it in paraffin and lit it, and held it under and along the feed pipe to thaw it all out. I got in the cab, loosened of the nut connection to the jets, turned the starter, the diesel came out. I had to connect it back up whilst switching the engine on, and away we went down to Stratford market.

I parked up in the market, placed my orders, with my regular wholesalers, went looking for some bargains, saw a mate of mine, and because it was so cold he had on this new ankle length fur coat which you couldn't help noticing.

He stopped at one of the shops and before he knew what was happening, there was a few of us in a line, hand resting on the one in front's shoulder, with the fur coat in front still not knowing, until we all started to sing *Underneath the Arches*, (by Flanagan and Allen) at 4.30 am in the morning.

I went back to my van in a somewhat in a better frame of mind, but the ******* thing would not start – it had frozen up again. So out came the rag, same as before. This happened five times along the road before the battery finally ran dry, directly on the corner of the Leytonstone High Road junction at traffic lights to Church street.

The worst possible place to break down, it was now seven in the morning, I'd been up all night on the roof shifting snow and ice, tipping buckets in the freezing cold, damp, hungry, tired, whacked out, beaten.

I looked up at the heavens and said, 'OK, you've beaten me.' And as I lowered my weary eyes, I saw it. There was a mini cab office, with a small sign saying *van for hire* (is it a game or does someone, or something, play games with us to see how much we can take?). I was on the move again; I ran into the mini cab office, signed up for half a day's hire, paid with a cheque I knew would bounce, unloaded all the sacks, boxes etc from one van to the hired one and shot home as fast as I could. Later the same day, I got the cheque back and paid cash.

Bobbie had already opened up properly two hours later than usual and I was not going to go through that again, so we decided to sell the business.

Talking about Bobbie, almost missed out our wedding photo.
Here we are in 1961.

This picture was taken of a young man I was asked to serve by a teacher from a school for deaf children who regularly brought in several children, one at a time, to help them get confidence.
I was happy to help.

Chapter 6

The Astral Plane

After selling up, we thought we'd buy a house and go on Holiday. We were living in a rented house in Derby Road, South Woodford – which we were lucky to get from a friend – and decided to go on holiday to Tenerife, taking along Debbie's friend Pearl.

Looking back it was our best holiday ever, maybe because Debbie was growing up fast, and that was the end of her childhood.

Once back from holiday, I had a couple of options as to what to do. I had an offer from a friend I had made who owned the Country Farm Shop at Epping. He sold about a hundred different items: jams, marmalades, potted creams, salads, garden furniture, sheds and logs as well as fruit and veg.

He had some goats, horses, chickens, ducks and some lovely white doves and a man-made pond, and asked me if I was interested in building and running a similar shop in a barn with outer buildings in Hainault Essex.

I would do what I was good at, buying from the main markets in Covent Garden, Stratford and Spitafields, and he would franchise me with the farm goods.

Another option was, whilst booking my holiday, the owner Tony Herbert who knew I had the fruit and veg shop across the road from his shop, asked me what my plans were.

He explained he needed some cash to help build his business and, if I was interested, to get in touch with him after my holiday.

After serious perusal over which was not an easy choice, I decided to put some money into the travel agents and mini cab service which Tony, with new cash injected, was re-opening. And so I became a Travel Agent.

Selling holidays was a piece of cake, everyone who came into the shop, on average, was likely to spend £200 to £300. We got 5% of all bookings, having to split commissions with large ABTA travel agents, mainly because we did not have ABTA which was not all bad, because it allowed us to sell bucket seats, cheap flights, which – excuse the pun – was just getting off the ground. You could say the business was on a high.

And coming back down to earth, the mini cab service was taking off; in fact the whole business was looking up. A lot of my old customers found their way into my new business and used the car service.

We applied, and got permission to sell British Rail tickets after I attended a British Rail course at Liverpool Street. After two weeks we were all set up.

Apart from holidays, the mini cab service and British Rail, we sold life insurance, travel insurance and coach tickets. We did printing and photocopying, and we introduced a membership club and ski club.

We printed a monthly magazine, and everyone who used any of our outlets became a free member. We called ourselves Astral Travel and the Astral mini cab service.

The name *Astral* came from my partner's hobby, and in fact his whole life. It was decided to bring in two new partners with some more cash. Surprisingly enough, everyone wanted to become part of the action and, unbeknown to me, Tony was on the astral plane forming partnerships with anybody.

It all came to an end when I received a phone call from a guy that I'd never met or even heard of, asking for Tony or myself. It turned out that he was a director of a well-known airline company and said that we – Tony, myself and another lady director – had signed an agreement to sell 20 flights a week with his company, and that he'd received no money.

He threatened to send the fraud squad in within 3 hours if we did not pay him £12,000 by the close of business.

Tony paid up, but I and the other partner decided to draw a line under the business account at the bank, to stop Astral trading.

The bank manager said it was unwise and that the company was doing well, but we decided to cut off our noses in spite of our faces, there being no trust in Tony left. Also, we did not know what else he was capable of. So I found myself, out of work, skint, and homeless.

I finished up going to the council, who thankfully gave us a lovely flat in Snaresbrooke.

My daughter Debbie was 15, which prompted the council to find us a home in the area. I got myself a night job for a security company, which I did until I was offered a job back at Barclays.

Me and Bobbie at a Ladies Night

Chapter 7

Back at the Eagle

My re-entry into Barclays Bank was helped by a good friend of ours, Roy Brown, whom I'd known since starting at the bank first time round.

I had to write a letter asking for a job and he at once got me an entry form which I filled in. Without further ado I got the job after a quick interview. Roy Brown actually interviewed me with his Manager of Staff present.

I'd signed a letter when I first left the bank stating I could never be re-employed, but that was with Barclays Ltd, I was re-employed by Barclays International. The date was set, and I returned to the bank with my tail between my legs – but life goes on.

Back at the bank, I was sent to Bullion for a short time, and then there was a chance of a branch job so I applied, through Roy Brown, and got the job.

The branch was in Holborn, Kingsway, Africa House, just across the road from Freemasons Hall and near to Lincoln Inns Fields, where I would spend my lunch breaks watching tennis, listening to the music entertainment or visiting the Charles Dickens Old Curiosity Shop.

I knew the area well; it was one of my old walks when I first worked for Barclays as a messenger. It had changed a lot since then. I think the main thing I miss was when I entered the buildings in Lincoln Inn. There used to be a large open fireplace, which in the winter was always alight. We would always go in for a warm, even if we had nothing to deliver or pick-up. Back in them days you could use this building as a short cut, in the front and out the back.

Old London was full of back alleys, and being on walks, we knew the City like the back of our hands; from Aldgate, Billingsgate, Newgate, Ludgate, Moorgate, Cripplegate to Bishopsgate – it was great to be back in the bank.

The builders were still in 54 Lombard Street, Barclays Head Office. I think they started rebuilding it when England won the World Cup in 1966 and had hardly finished it by 1990 when they decided to pull it down and start to build a greenhouse in place of one of the best buildings in London.

Inside head office (the old building) was a replica of the original room that was the start of Barclays Bank which was in 72 Cheapside, just along the road from, St Mary-Le-Bow (the sound of Bow bells and the Cockney story).

There was a wonderful theatre inside where the Barclay Operatic Society put on some top class shows. They had seating for 200 people, some first class cinema equipment and could raise the whole floor and seating to the ceiling, to leave a top class dance floor. In the basement at one time was a shooting gallery and two squash courts.

The banking hall was very large with beautiful marble. Rumour has it that Barclays, after ordering the marble from a quarry in Italy, decided to buy the quarry, get the marble at low cost price, and then sold the quarry on, making a large profit.

So the marble cost zilch and then, when the building was being rebuilt, I hear they sold the marble from the building to an ex-employee, the head cashier, who retired and now deals in reclaimed marble.

After a year at Africa house, I was offered a job at St Swithin's House, on the Elite security team. I jumped at the chance and after an interview with the St Swithin's management, I was accepted.

I teamed up with some old cronies from 54 Lombard Street, but was always made to feel an outsider – this I understood to a certain degree, but I was good at my job, and they knew it.

Maybe they thought I was after their jobs, this was not the case. I was still living at Snarsbrooke in a lovely flat but, unfortunately some elderly people above complained about Debbie, our daughter who was now 16 – 17, coming home late at night and making a noise.

We knew they were exaggerating, but could not carry on living in an upstairs flat, so we got a swap with an elderly couple in Black Horse Lane, Walthamstow, E17. The exchange was our 2 bedroom flat, for a 3 bedroom house, so we moved.

Soon after moving in, we applied for right to buy forms and in due course, brought the freehold property.

By this time I asked the bank if I could amalgamate my present service with my past (frozen) service and the staff department approved it. I received a letter to that affect. Soon after receiving the letter, I was summoned to see the manageress of security for my yearly report, and just by chance my service time was mentioned.

She took great pleasure in reminding me that my past service, which was frozen, could never be added to my present service. Little did she know that I had a letter in my pocket, confirming that past and present service had been amalgamated, but I did not spoil her day and kept quiet.

At this time Bobbie was working as a manageress for a dry cleaners shop in South Woodford, next to a shoe shop, and opposite Jets, the wine bar.

A young man used to come in and sit and chat to her, it was Warren Barton now playing for Newcastle. He'd played one game for England and I knew him at Watford, and would regularly pick him up from his house in Walthamstow to take him for training with Watford. He was always hanging around to see a girl called Candy whom he went on to marry. Candy was mates with the girl from the shoe shop and would regularly sit and talk to Bobbie.

I am so glad he managed to get into top flight football. I must confess I did not believe he would make it, and along with Dean and David Holdsworth, who were at school with Debbie my daughter, I watch him regularly on the telly.

They are just a few of the many excellent footballers who were with us at Watford. Incidentally, I stopped scouting for Watford after a disagreement with Steve Harrison, then Watford's youth coach and later with Millwall, and finally England with Graham Taylor.

Although we never had words or argued, I could never agree with Steve Harrison's actions in getting rid of 80% of the boys, myself and Ken Brooks another Watford scout, had scouted before even seeing them actually play a game of football.

Bobbie by then had packed up her job at the dry cleaners. She did not like working for the new owners and got herself a job doing school dinners. I think she liked the children calling her Miss. Debbie had left school and was working as a receptionist in Leytonstone.

Out of the blue, a rumour went around that St Swithins was closing and security staff was being offered voluntary redundancy.

The rumour was true and, sure enough, in September 1991 around came the offer. It took me all of five minutes to work out my final figure, remember two services – the first twelve and a half years, plus the second six and a half years (amalgamated) totalled 19 years. I thought that I was dreaming.

They were offering me a king's ransom; I would have to work three and a half life times, to save that amount up, so I made my appointment, requested voluntary redundancy and showed them my letter concerning my service record.

Once they confirmed my final figures and pension options, they asked me to sign a form stating that there would be no going back or changing my mind once signed. I could not sign quickly enough. I was leaving, a date was set – Feb 1992 – and I started to make plans.

On Christmas Eve I was summoned to the manager's office where the conversation went as follows.

'Thanks for coming in Mr Anthony. Mmm, sit down. I've been wrestling with a problem.' Pause. 'After consideration the question you see is, should I tell you now, and ruin your Christmas, or leave it to after Christmas?'

'If you have bad news, sir, tell me now as soon as possible, then I can sort it out,' I replied.

'You had better read this letter from head office.' And the letter read (I forget the exact words):

It is the bank's decision that the offer of voluntary redundancy has been withdrawn because of the break in your service.

It went on to say that I could re-apply for a lesser amount, which was nearly £20,000 less. The manager said that he was really sorry about this.

I asked about the letter I signed, stating that I could not change my mind.

'Well, head office feels,' the manager said, 'that on this occasion they will let you change your mind if you think the money on offer now is not to your liking.'

'I don't mean me going back on my word,' I answered back, 'I mean them. I understood the letter I signed meant that, both me and the bank had an agreement.'

'Ah, well. No,' the manager answered. 'You are the only one who signed any form. I must say you are taking this very well, now I really must go – last minute shopping presents. Merry Christmas.' and he showed me the door. I decided there and then that I would fight to the bitter end.

My options being if I took the revised lower offer, they would pay me one and a half years salary plus a small pension, or I could continue working in the bank for a very good wage, for about five or six years with a good pension at the end, and I would retire at the age of 60. The third option was of course getting the bank to honour what we had agreed.

Coming back to work after the Christmas break, everyone seemed to know about my knock back, and the consensus of opinion was that I would lose.

I was again called to the manager's office and asked my intentions about what I wanted to do.

I asked if him if the bank had re-considered their mistake and said that I was getting in touch with the staff association, which I did.

The staff association considered my case and referred me to a solicitor, who said she thought I had enough of a chance to get the bank to reconsider.

Four weeks later, after much haggling, with letters being sent to and fro, they made me a offer which I at once asked for time to consider, well knowing that if I could delay them for a few weeks my pay was going to be increased. I was due another yearly increment which would move my final figures on par with the same as what was first offered. Plus, of course, I had two extra month's pay.

Add to this the solicitor's fees and I feel the bank lost out, which was not what I wanted, because apart from the few silly people that you will always get, Barclays Bank are the best employers, and from the conversations I heard over the dining tables in the ante rooms, and in all business I have had with them over 35 years, they are the most trustworthy and honest bank.

So there I was again, out of work and 55 years of age with a mortgage. But I did have a kings ransom which I was frightened to use, and was being escorted off the premises of St Swithin's House, which they do it being a computer centre.

So I walked for 3 hours, putting my name down in every job centre and agency I could find from the bank all the way down through to Holborn, and then on to Oxford Street and on up to Regent Street.

The following day I sent my CV to the addresses I had visited, and others from out of the Yellow Pages, then sat back waiting for the phone to ring.

Judging by the response I had, and at a time when it seemed politically correct to have three to four million people out of work – don't ask me why – I appeared to have no trouble whatsoever in getting a job, and in no time at all I was working again. Also, I was being offered other jobs at the same time.

I had previously applied for a live-in caretaker / porter's job in

Bryanstone Square, Marble Arch, W1. I went for the interview and was offered the job. Since leaving the bank I had bought an old house in Goldsmith Road, Walthamstow, E17 – just two streets away from where we were living in Blackhorse Lane.

We were doing it up to sell on, or rent out. Bobbie was working as a school dinner lady, and as I already said, enjoyed the job and liked to be called Miss again.

Debbie was married by then and was quite happy living in Leytonstone with her hubby Barry. It was quite a wrench, but we decided to have a go and see how things would work out. Bobbie reluctantly left the school dinner's job and off we went to a live in the centre of London's West End.

I soon settled into the job and got to know the owners and tenants of the 98 flats we were to look after.

The flats at that time, 1993, were selling for about £500,000 each, so I estimated our flat, on the ground floor was worth about £200,000.

I found myself living in a luxury flat, paying no rent, rates, electricity, heating or telephone bills and being paid a fair wage. I also owned a three bedroom house in Walthamstow plus a two bedroom cottage with no fares or any other out goings. So I decided to let out both properties, and sit back.

I did have to live among Lords, Ladies, Counts and Countesses and millionaires as neighbours, but you cannot have everything.

The job was not without any problems from the inmates, as I called them. One that comes to mind was from Lady Smith, the wife of Roland Smith (Manchester United) who lived in one of the apartments.

She came to my flat complaining that the people upstairs were arguing and shouting, warned me that there might be a murder, and suggested that I should go up and ask them to stop their noise. I suggested that I should give them a short time to have their row and get it out of their system.

After ten minutes Lady Smith returned saying that I should not allow it to go on any longer and that I should go up and either tell them to stop, or ask them to row in English so that she and her neighbours could establish what was going on. I went up and knocked, and was told to mith off in Creek.

Another tenant who complained about a different noise asked me to go to his neighbours and give them a tape, and ask them not to turn the music up loud when they argued. If they did though, would they play the tape that I gave them because he hated their country music that they turned up loud when arguing. It was driving him mad. The tape he gave me to play was Barry Manilow.

Another awkward duty I was asked to perform was waking up the Countess. She was writing a book and found that she could concentrate more at night, without any phone calls or any interruptions. She slept in the afternoon, so I was asked to wake her up late afternoon to early evening. I had to go up to her apartment, let myself in, and wake her up.

Trouble was, she wore earplugs and an eye mask to keep out the noise and the light; so it was difficult to wake her up, without shaking her bed.

The inevitable happened. Into the bedroom I strolled, and there she was, in the wrong posture with her husband who apparently had been given the job of waking her up. The funny thing was though, she was still wearing her earplugs and eye mask!

Dame Felicity Peake MBE lived on the first floor, and true to the words in her book, *Pure Chance,* she found it easy to get along with people such as porters, doormen, cleaners, chauffeurs, and the like. A wonderful person, and I can imagine her in wartime at Biggin Hill (Susanna York portrayed her in the film *The Battle of Britain*) getting on with the job, and generally getting the best out of all those about her. I will always remember her at the age of 80; it seemed immediately after her hip operation there she was on her own, three times a day walking around Bryanstone Square, (approximately half a mile).

I used to keep my eye on her, just in case she had an accident, but after a few days she was flying about (she would love that expression, anything to do with aircraft). Bobbie and I were more than happy to attend her 80th birthday gathering at the War Memorial Museum, which she used to launch her book, *Pure Chance*, in aid of charity. There was me, mingling with all the famous film stars, actors and air force officers.

Here we are at Dame Felicity Peake's book launch at the War Memorial Museum

Returning to Bryanstone Square, which I was told was taken over during the war and used as headquarters for the American, General Pattern. But back to 1993, along with the others I mentioned in Bryanstone Square were a Prince, a Sheikh, an army general and a certain Mr Prager (Mickey Duff) the boxing promoter, a very nice man with a mischievous sense of humour,

He had a cleaner who came in once a week, took his shirts to the cleaners and would collect those from the previous week. The cleaner came to me crying and very worried, apparently Mickey was three shirts short, and getting rather shirty about it. It reminded me of Humphrey Bogart, with the strawberry jam fiasco in the film *The Cane Mutiny*.

I said that I would look for the shirts to get the cleaner out of the jam, but could not find any. I was surprised to find that Mickey had 20 or 30 other shirts, many new and not even used. He was adamant that the shirts were missing. In the end the shirts were discovered at the cleaners.

We were not sure what really happened, but we think his wife had taken them there. The cleaner was very upset, and we heard no more from her.

I became good friends with Malcolm and Barbara Beattie, who worked in the next building as caretakers, Malcolm was a Scotsman, but emigrated to New Zealand at the age of 40, way back in the 1960s. The reason I believe he left was because he was fed up with all of the Scottish goalkeepers.

He had married Barbara, a lovely New Zealand girl. They have three bairns, now all grow up. So he decided to return to the UK thirty years later, to see if there had been any improvements (none). Although to hear him speak you had never know he had been away.

He used to call me Magnet and said if I were to stand still long enough I would become a millionaire owing to the fact that every time he saw me, some-one was giving me a tip. This is true; I went to a new shop in Edgware Road to get some keys cut. They also sold ornaments, lighting, etc. I told the man that I looked after 100 flats (trying to get a discount), and he said if I recommended his shop to the tenants, I could have my keys cut for nothing, and he gave £10 as well.

Sometime later, Malcolm came to see me with a sheepish look on his face. He was embarrassed.

'I don't know how to tell you this Dan,' he said, 'but I guess you'll find out from Barbara. One of my tenants held out a £20 note for a tip. I said to him, as you would ...' (trying to get me to agree with him before I heard what he had to say), 'No that's all right, so he put it back in his pocket.'

'You clown,' I said, 'you're supposed to snatch it out of his hand, put it in your pocket, then say thanks very much, you did not really have to.'

I then added to Malcolm, 'You're just like your goalkeepers; they let everything slip through their hands, too.' It's funny what makes people feel good about themselves, and I'm no exception.

I was at Cheshunt, Spurs old training ground. I'd taken along two of my nephews to watch Watford boys play Spurs boys. Just as we were approaching the dressing rooms, two old chaps who were standing, chatting, said to me, 'Hello, Danny, what did you think of the game on Saturday?' Watford had beaten Everton 2-0, so I went over and chatted to them for ten minutes.

The nephews said to me, 'Who were they, Dan?'

'Oh, just two blokes asking my opinion,' said I proudly. I had just been talking to the two men who, at that time, were the only ex-managers to have won the F.A. cup and First Division championship in the same season.

The gentlemen are icons in the football world, Berti Mee with Arsenal

1988, and Bill Nicholson with Spurs 1960. The records will show others have achieved the Double since.

Wapping Pier Head, 1960

Chapter 8

Going to Mayfair, 1993

It was in the summer of 1993. I was asked to receive a number of boxes from Christie's, and make sure they were safely put into flat number 2, Bryanstone Square, owned by a Mr Petie. We had agreed to clean the flat once a week, and generally looked after it allowing visitors of theirs to use the flat from time to time. A London based manager/accountant would contact me of any prior arrangements. One day he came to Bryanston Square and asked me if I knew (being in the caretaker business) anybody I could recommend for a job similar to what I already did, but of a smaller scale. I asked more about the job and was told they were looking for a couple simply to live in a house in Mayfair and make it secure.

It seemed like a dream job that comes along once in a lifetime and I said that I knew just the chap for such a job, – ME! 'We hoped you would say that,' said the manager, 'as soon as the building has been redecorated and had new building works done, you can look it over.' Bobbie was quite happy about leaving Bryanston Square. She was not paid a wage but obviously lived in the flat with me rent free.

She had no job contract but was expected to cover for me if I was elsewhere in the building. So when we had a chance to move away, she looked forward to it.

Bobbie's sister, Ena, had died in 1992, and then rather suddenly Ena's husband, Tom Murray, died. They were both very close to us and Bobbie took it very badly. On top of having to leave her job serving school dinners, Bobbie became very ill. I took her to the doctor who examined her but said she could not find anything wrong.

Bobbie was losing a lot of weight, she was not drinking or eating, and she seemed to have a lot of pain in her mouth and face. I took her back to the doctor and was told that we should go to the dentist regarding the pain in her mouth.

After seeing the dentist, who also said that he could see nothing wrong, Bobbie was getting worse, and losing more weight. I had my suspicions as to what was wrong and told the doctor whom I called in to see her for the third time. I said I could smell cancer, the same smell as Bobbie's sister Ena had, but the doctor said no. She thought that I mollycoddled Bobbie too much but, to put my mind at rest, she would make an appointment for the hospital.

I'd had enough and looked through the yellow pages, to get another opinion. Very shortly a doctor arrived and, after just looking at Bobbie for a minute or two, beckoned me outside. He asked if my heart was strong (he was very blunt). I said I thought it was okay, and he told me to expect the worst. He told me that Bobbie had cancer and suggested I got her into hospital the same day.

I gave him his £75.00 fee, and away he went leaving me in complete shock, not really knowing what to do. I phoned my GP at once, but being a Saturday, I got put through to an answer phone. I dashed across the square to a private clinic – again no joy – come back on Monday, I was told. Then I phoned a private hospital and found out that you've got to have previously joined; it's no good waiting until you are ill.

I phoned the local hospital and was told I would have to make an appointment through my GP. I was distraught (there it goes again, it's got to be some kind of a game, you are brought to your knees). You don't know where or which way to turn and then you remember a brief conversation you had with one of the tenants concerning his son having become the top man at Charring Cross hospital in Hammersmith.

So up I rush to Mr Theodora's flat, Number 16 – I had to try it. I rang the doorbell. He came to the door and I just could not speak. I was completely overcome, emotionally drained.

He took me in, sat me down and tried to get me to tell him what was wrong. He phoned his son and told me to go back down to Bobbie who was just lying in bed, very weak, awaiting her fate.

Mr Theodora's son came and told us not to take any notice of the advice from the previous doctor or GP that had attended Bobbie. We were told to go to the Charring Cross hospital on the following Monday. He did one test and at once told us that Bobbie would be admitted to carry out further tests. We took her up to the ward and tried to make her comfortable.

The tests took five days to discover that Bobbie was suffering from Non Hodgekin's Lymphoma. Once they knew what was wrong, they knew how to treat her. The following morning Professor Newlands and his team took over. They decided that Bobbie should receive 26 weeks chemotherapy followed by radiotherapy.

Following many months of uncertainty Bobbie recovered, thank God, and has decided to stick around because she had not finished shopping. We were thinking of moving aboard because there are shops there that she has not brought anything from. But give her time and she'll get around to all of them.

If you've never looked after anyone on chemotherapy and held down a live-in caretaker's job at the same time, you cannot imagine how I came to give Bobbie a double dose of steroid tablets – 40 tablets instead of 20. By this time, the 6th or 7th week of therapy, Bobbie was down to five and a half stones, half her normal body weight. I had been up half the night making sure she took her pills at exactly the correct time. She was still hardly eating or drinking anything and each pill had to be crushed up. I should explain; she had to take 37 pills a day, 20 of them being steroids. She had thrush on her tongue, had lost all the hair on her body and laid about looking like Ghandi (no disrespect to the famous man).

Then at 7.00am the buzzer went off. Bobbie was trying to be sick so I rushed to the intercom, one of the tenants (inmates), very rich, 80 years of age, wanted me to phone the paper shop to find out why her *Financial Times* had not arrived.

She just had to know how her shares were doing. I said I would find out and phoned the paper shop, but alas I could not get through. Half the population of Westminster was phoning for the same reason I suppose, but my tenant must have buzzed down a dozen times. It, or him, was playing the game again, pushing me to the limit. I don't mind myself being tried but this was affecting Bobbie.

With the postman late as well, my tenant was going mad – no paper, no mail. Well, it all resulted in me giving Bobbie a double dose of steroids. Once I realised what I'd done, I thought I'd killed her and phoned the hospital straight away. Fortunately the hospital said it was not too bad, and to miss the next day's dosage. That's the time I decided to leave Bryanstone Square.

After Bobbie's 26 week chemotherapy course had ended and the lumps in her neck had been reduced to zero, radiotherapy followed; she was on the road to recovery. The wonderful work of all at the hospital, the security guards and all the staff up to the main man, had given her back to us.

Going back a few years a strange thing happened to us. It's weird the way it happened. My niece was getting engaged and was talking to us about what kind of ring she wanted. The very next day at work – I was still at the bank at that time – a colleague said that somebody had these rings for sale. I said my niece might be interested and I was given a ring to show her. I took a quick look and put the ring, which was in a nice small box, into my pocket. That evening we had previously arranged to take my other niece, Dawn, to see a faith healer.

On the way to the healer's home in Limehouse, we stopped off to show Margaret the ring. She decided she did not like it and we went on to Limehouse. Bobbie had a quick look and said she might like to keep it.

We arrived at Freddie the faith healers house and in we went. Bobbie and Dawn went upstairs with Freddie, I was left downstairs with Freddie's wife who, it turns out, was a clairvoyant.

We sat talking, and of course the subject of her work came up. After a while I was convinced that she was not all the ticket. She said that she worked closely with the police and even produced cuttings from out of a paper, detailing how she led the police to Millwall dock's entrance and found the body of a boy that had gone missing for weeks.

She went on to tell me that she had film stars and business clients who regularly sent her letters with personal items enclosed for her to hold and give them readings. She then started to talk about a lucky ring and I realised she was describing the ring in my pocket. At this point the others came into the room, and I said to them, 'Listen to this,' and asked her to repeat what she had just said. I got the ring out of my pocket and this lady described every detail of the ring in my hand, without seeing it.

'Whatever you do,' she said, 'keep that ring. You will find it will bring you a lot of luck.' Still holding the ring, she started asking questions.

'Who is Kate?' and then said, 'I can see a lot of people rowing, something to do with pigeons, and washing on a line.'

All of this meant little to me until a week later my sister Mary told me that our aunt Betty and our grandfather were continually rowing with the next door neighbours concerning their pigeons messing all over the cloths line. We decided to keep the ring.

I have always thought us quite lucky and I always wonder if it was the good doctors, chemotherapy, or the lucky ring that pulled Bobbie through that horrible disease. We still wonder how Fred's wife, described that ring.

Soon after, the Mayfair job turned up. Bobbie's hair was beginning to grow again and she wanted another wig. So back to Paddington we went, to the shop, (now a hairdresser) that I told you about earlier, the very shop

I visited with my uncle Bill, 50 years before.

I thought at once, what would the funny handshake brotherhood think if they knew? I had joined 5 years earlier but found it very difficult what with looking after Bobbie, holding down my job and finding time to make and write speeches. It showed in one toast I did for the founders and past masters. I thought I would praise them for all the good work carried out over the years through the Industrial Revolution, two World Wars, two minor setbacks – called recessions – and one major setback called John. It went down like a lead balloon so I added a quick ad-lib, or if you're a cricket nut like me, Shane Warne. Ha! Just when you think you're getting ahead, he comes up with a googly, that's Shane Warne not John Major. It did raise a few eyebrows.

When the Mayfair job came up, which had been offered approximately one year earlier, I was asked if I could meet the owners at the Connaught Hotel, on the corner of Mount Street, W1. Mr and Mrs Petti, who were Italians, were staying at the hotel.

Along we went with Bobbie in her wig; the meeting went well and a date was arranged for us to move in. They asked my advice as to what part of the house I would like to live in, and agreed that the ground floor, and not the top floor, would be better for security and reception purposes. So ground floor at the back of the house it was.

The address is Mount Row, Mayfair, London, W1. A grade II listed building comprising of six bedrooms, eight bathrooms, three kitchens, two large lounges, one large dining room, a specially built sun lounging room at the top of the roof, two garages, and a basement bedroom with a gothic style ceiling and a hide-a-way tryst with ornate fountains and statuettes (and a partridge in a pear tree!!). It also had gardens at the rear, complete with night-lights, lanterns and dimmer switches. Berkeley Square (with no nightingales singing), where I used to clean up after the Ball, was less than two minutes away.

Nicky Clarke's Hairdressers was just around the corner. At the end of the row was Vivian Westwood's dress shop, in Davis Street, for Bobbie to get a nice cheap dress to go with her wig.

Our next door neighbour was Paula Yates and all her lovely children. They lived in this rather strange building with a roof garden and the children with Paula or their nanny was always playing and laughing. When they moved away Cher moved in. Quite different neighbours from what one had in Hedworth Street. Bow, E3.

The house in Mount Row was quite weird in a way, with large fireplace surrounds built in a Medieval/Gothic style. It had rams heads, swine, and elf like faces all over it.

Bobbie never really felt at ease alone in the house with all its grandeur; the beautiful large wooden staircase going up the middle of the house, its marble bathrooms, columns, and fabric walls, its bedrooms with their walls lined in real silk, each carefully designed, one for the master and one for the dame by an interior designer, and furnished to their personnel likings.

We were offered the same treatment but Bobbie declined – she wanted our own furniture. Our living room was 36 feet long and 18 feet wide with French doors to the garden and four large windows. It was fully panelled (with a hidden door to the utility room), had a wooden floor and the ceiling had six large panels of plaster, each with scenes from the *Fountain of Youth*. They were being taken away and stored when the building was being renovated. Apparently the six panels were why the building was grade two listed.

In the 14 months we were there, the owners only slept there for one solitary night. The rest of the time Bobbie and I cleaned, secured, and generally kept the house looking as if it was lived in. We switched the lighting on and off to show the house was occupied. The only other duty I had, was receiving antiques from Christie's and Sotheby's.

There we were, living in the heart of Mayfair, near Park Lane, one of the best addresses in the world. We were paying no rent, rates, and had no other out goings. But Bobbie did not like it there; she was not allowed to hang washing on the line. She was not even allowed to have a line – one of the local council rules! Has the Queen got a royal line? Also, every time I went to buy a newspaper, prostitutes plying their trade stopped me. I was reading 20 newspapers a day. (Only kidding).

They would also brazenly knock on the door, ring the bell, and make out to ask for somebody. When asked their business, they would openly tell you. I suppose living there, they thought I owned it. So we decided to leave at the end of December, 1996. Bobbie was still visiting the hospital but her hair had grown again.

We brought a house near to Debbie in Purfleet, Essex, and I rang up the job agency. In no time at all I was working again, this time in my old back yard, Dundee Court, Wapping High Street, E1. A stranger could be excused if he could not find the High Street, it reminded me of the two hours I spent looking for the beaches at Carshalton. I did not know where to stick my snorkel when I found out Carshalton Beeches were trees and not sand dunes.

I was to look after an old warehouse/flat. Of course the memories came flooding back, Christmas 1956/7 when I was working with a guy called Roy Gill. He was an ex-boxer but still did a bit of sparring at Terry Spinks place in Canning Town. We were doing building repairs in Dundee Court, near Morocco Wharf (now a police boat yard), mainly glazing, and that's what caused a spot of trouble. We had just re-glazed four panels of glass and Roy was not at all pleased with the crane driver who was unloading three wheeled, two seater bubble cars. We were paid so much for every pane completed but unfortunately the crane driver had either lost his glasses or was already in the Christmas spirit, or he'd been sacked by Spinksy's, the demolition firm from Dagenham, because it seemed he was trying to demolish Morocco Wharf with the bubble cars.

The building was being hit more times than Rocky Marciano had hit Don Cockle (what a fight that was, I watched it at the Regal Cinema near Bow Church). Now Roy did not mind what he was doing to the building, but Roy's bubble burst when our four panes of glass were broken, especially before the putty has dried. The row nearly caused a strike by the dockers but they found a compromise by smashing a dozen windows that we could easily replace, and recover our loses.

Dundee Court had changed beyond all recognition. Its name for a start was St John's Wharf. At that time, Wapping was full up with lorries and carts during the week, and the noisy cranes, and shouting from the dockers was endless.

One of my former jobs was at Robert Hough, now called the Paper mill. Robert Hough collected, sorted and made paper. I can remember going to Harrods warehouse near Fulham, a massive warehouse with a large basement, which you could drive an eight wheeler into.

We went there to collect these large crates of religious photographs, thousands of them, roughly 3ft by 2ft. All mounted on thick white card, they were all cut-up and put into a large vat, boiled down to a mash, and rolled into large rolls of paper.

I worked on the top floor where the paper was off loaded from lorries and pulled up by crane. I used to pull the paper in, stack it in piles, and then pour out and spread each sack onto a large table with half a dozen girls each side grading – that is picking out and sorting the waste paper. Then they put it in different sacks, colours in one bag and whites in another.

Paper Mill is now luxury flats and that top sorting room is now selling for £750,000 upwards. The same building where a man called Horse used to carry half hundred weight bales of waste paper up a small flight of stairs, and another bloke used to come daily to see if there were any old bits of rope, chains, driftwood, iron, anything to sell on, and make some kind of living.

He actually lived on an old boat, which looked like the African Queen, but not in such good condition. Down the road from Hough's was the Grapes, one of the oldest pubs on the river. Daniel Farson, a writer and television presenter, lived a few doors away above a onetime barge builder's workshop before moving to his music hall pub on the Isle of Dogs. Next door to the Grapes, lived Dr. David Owen, MP for Labour before becoming one of the famous four Liberal Democrats. He bought an old rundown house for about two shillings, (old money) in the early 1960s. I have always been of the opinion that there are people who can see into the future because, by the time I came back to Wapping in 1996, there were film stars, footballers, show business and pop stars, all rushing to buy old houses nearly 30 years too late.

I work now in Dundee Court, next to St Patrick's School, the very same school my uncle Gus, (remember the Charrington's beer lorry) attended when he was a small boy and lived just off Wapping Lane. St Patrick's is a part of Wapping's history and now they are thinking of making it into flats or something worse, maybe a new mint (not royal) to print the Euro.

Wapping has changed so much since the 1960s; the smell of the warehouses, the spices, tea, sugar, and thousands of other aromas.

The groups of dockers working away loading and unloading barges – 2000 tonnes a day, by hand in gangs of 10 and 12. The sound of tugs, ships, double docked, the thousands of barges made it look as if you could walk across the Thames stepping from one barge to another.

The long, long wait when the bridges were raised to allow the ships into the docks, past Pierhead, and across the High Street. You could reach out your hand and touch them, as they drifted by and you could see the faces of the crewmen. They waved down to you, eager and happy to be back on dry land after weeks at sea. Even now I smile to myself when I see the different kinds of people at Wapping station, much different to the hoards of dockers and stevedores (no, nothing to do with bullfighting) that regularly had to walk up and down the stairs because the lift was out of order. No changes there, they still are.

I was coming home from work one night just approaching Wapping station, when I saw an old pal that I used to work with called Hammersly, one of two brothers. We'd all worked for Unity Ashfelt, a firm based in Stratford, E14.

They were roofers and the last time that I had seen them, I was at Three Mill Lane, Bromley-by-Bow. We had been working in one of the remaining mills, in a building that made Alka Seltza.

'How's your Rolls-Royce?' I shouted over, and we both laughed. The story is, in 1957 when hardly anybody had a car, he and his brother told us that they had brought a Rolls Royce and that their girlfriends had been out in it and, of course, they'd had a lovely time in the back.

Well, they carried on for weeks about this car, but no one had seen it. Our boss also heard about it, he could not understand how they could afford a Roller, especially as he only had an old Ford. He must be paying them too much. Next morning we were all sitting in the café and in they came.

'The Roller's out the front,' they shouted and we all ran outside to look. True enough it was a Roller. It was an old hearse complete with the rollers (for the coffins) in the back.

'You didn't do it with her on the rollers, do you?' asked the boss. 'Yes,' answered one brother, and the other one said, 'He had to stop halfway through to oil the rollers.'

'Did it come with a coffin?' asked someone else. 'Of cause it did; we keep our tools in that!' they replied.

I went over to have a chat, and asked him if he still had the Roller, and asked after his brother.

'He died years ago and had his last ride in a Roller,' he said. 'Oh, by the way, this is his son Roy, you know, short for Royce. That's because he was ...'

'Yes,' I said, 'don't embarrass the lad, I get the picture.'

I could not help but smile to myself, and even on the train all the way home, I was getting strange looks. I must have been laughing out loud. I was thinking, what would his dad have called him if he'd been conceived in a Cadillac, Daimler or Lotus? Cad, Dame or Lotty? I suppose if he'd been conceived in a Taxi they'd have called him Cab!

Now, at the age of 64, I suppose I'll not be starting any new careers so I'll just have to live with my memories.

I'm proud to be English and was born in London, England. My early days in Camden town, NW1, was no different to any other kid. By 1938, when I was born, the Irish had already been around long enough to influence the names of myself and my brothers and sisters. I can just about remember a Greek or Cypriot boy named Tassas, who was different to the other kids. At my school, Richard Cobden, there must have been kids talking different languages but I do not recall.

I remember my dad making leather handbags and sandals for a Greek or Cypriot man in North London, Camden Road. My dad was teaching my mum and she was stitching by hand, of course we had no electricity in those days.

I can remember later my uncle Bill getting himself locked up by the police for throwing bricks at a group of Cypriots who were marching down Camden High Street shouting, 'Give us back our country.' And my grandfather, William Anthony, being escorted from Woolworth's by a policeman because they would not give him back his money for an item he had brought. Not knowing that it had been made in Japan until he had returned home, he rushed back to Woolworth's wearing his war medals and making one hell of a scene.

And I'll never forget the long hot summers, spent with mum and my aunts Katie and Betty, (my dad's sisters) playing around in Regent's Park or the cricket match for the school when I carried my bat (that's being the opening batsman, not being out at the end of the innings). And you know, if I live to be one hundred, I'll not forget every goal I ever scored, (there wasn't that many!). I retired early at 39, after playing on most bits of turf in London.

I was lucky enough to play for 33 seasons, most games at Hackney Marshes. I kid you not, you had to book up one year in advance to get the privilege to play there and be sure of a getting a pitch. They were the days when you could talk to a ref; and nobody could kick the ball to the halfway line as it was made of leather, hand stitched, laced up, with the end tucked in. Every time you headed it you felt your head, to see if you still had one.

I can re-live every fight I had, the one when my mum pulled me off the toughest boy in the neighbourhood. There I was, 8 years old, sitting on top of this bully, raining blows to his head and body, and mum stopped it. He always claimed that he would have finished on top but we'll never know. He never picked a fight with me again, and I certainly did not want to fight him again. And then, in later years when I was about 14, there was Furgy

Murphy. Furgy, short for Furgus had a bit of a reputation as a hard nut; he always went around with a crowd and we always used to cross over the road to avoid him.

Well, my brother Terry would not cross the road for anybody, and Terry told Furgy that I bash him up if he were to touch him. The first I heard about it was when Furgy's gang surrounded me; there was no way out. Luckily enough for me, Furgy was not as tough as he thought he was, and after I'd downed him a couple times, one of the parents came over and stopped the fight, and made us shake hands. But that's life, up and down like Tower Bridge, one long battle.

I look out of Dundee Court, down Wapping high Street, less than five minutes away from Tower Bridge, and the Tower of London, at St Catherine's dock (with a bit of sun, much better than Marbella's Porto Banus). I turn my head the other way to see the police boatyard, but remember Morocco Wharf. What a waste, knocking it down. It could have been turned into another 50 apartments.

I think of the café on wheels in the gardens, near to the back of Morocco Wharf, ran by Ma Sullivan. Then there was the Abbott's Tea Rooms at the top of Wapping Lane owned by my Uncle John, Gus Abbott's brother (remember Gus on the Charrington's lorry, 55 years ago?). They are all gone now, but not forgotten, closed down along with Mables at Tower Bridge, when all the dockers left. They were near to the only sandy beach up until the age of 20, I'd been on; all 1,500 tons of sand, put there with the approval of King George V in June 1934, and guaranteed free access for ever – that is unless the common market overlords decide to interfere, Of course, that's not counting Southend-On -Sea.

I jokingly say that I dragged Bobbie, out of Bow but, she quickly replies, 'I got him from off the back of a lorry.' And I think she's joking, when she adds, 'I should have left him there!'

Bobbie with her two sisters

DEDICATION

To my daughter Debbie whose grandparents died when she was very young.
I hope this book gives her some insight as to her roots.

Danny

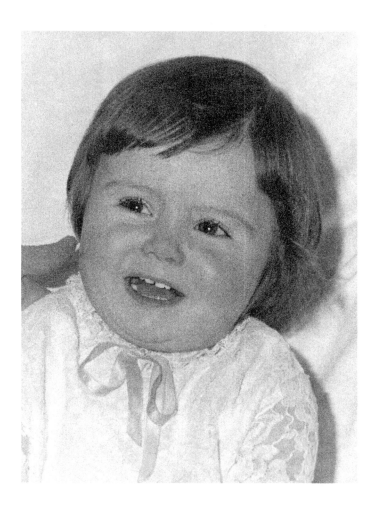

ACKNOWLEDGEMENTS

My thanks to Tammie Smith who encouraged me to write more, and to my daughter Debbie Johnson for her help which has always been appreciated.

And not forgetting my bosses over the years – 34 at the last count – including my current boss who remains the only one to whom I've yet to say, 'Lick 'em and stick 'em!'
   (Lick 'em and stick 'em is the polite way of saying you can stick your job anywhere you choose *BUT* make sure the Insurance Stamps are appropriately stuck on, and up to date, when you give me my P45 and final pay.)

My thanks also to Susan Hamilton and everyone at Dundee Court in Wapping who helped make the 1st edition of this book possible.

To Vickie and Terry. Thank you. I am really impressed with all your hard work, help and ideas for the 2nd edition which are 'nihil nisi optimum' (nothing but the best). Thank you both.
   Danny Anthony, a true Londoner.

REFLECTION OF BOBBIE ABBOTT'S LIFE

To my dear wife Roberta who came into my life in 1947, outside the Mile End hospital, Bancroft Road Stepney.
There she was sitting in the driver's cab of the brewery lorry, next to her father and the driver. They were going on a day trip delivering beer into Southend on sea.

Bobbie would not have believed that not only would she marry the scruffy boy who was sitting on the crates on the back of the lorry with his uncle Gus, but she would be coming back to the same hospital in 23 year's time, to have his baby Deborah. Or that on the way to Southend, they would stop and deliver beer to a pub called "The Barge".
I cannot believe that 76 years from 1947 to 2023, that I would be writing this true story in the same room that Bobbie died in, which was in a bungalow called Riverview Court, next door to "The Barge", with me sitting by her bed, holding her hand. Bobbie's last word was "Mum".
None of this could have happened if not for destiny, and that this story was not dreamt up by some old man.

Its origin began in 1904, in a Welsh mining village called Merthyr Tydfil. When a very young girl named Margaret Llewellyn was taken on holiday by her uncle and aunt.

Fast forward to 1924, Margaret Caswell now 20 years old, met Tom Abbott and wanted to get married to him. Margaret's parents objected as they thought Tom, a sailor, was not the right person for her.
Tom and Margaret would not be put off and her parents refused to provide her birth certificate.
So they went to Somerset House to get a copy, and discovered that Mr. and Mrs. Caswell did not have any children. The truth was out?
Margaret was please to know that she had one brother and three sisters in Merthyr Tydfil.

Tom and Margaret got married, moved into No.8 Knapp Road in Bow E3 where they had a son and 4 daughters. Unfortunately Tom and Margaret both passed before 1960.
The youngest daughter Roberta met Danny in 1960 and they were married in 1962 where they then moved into 8 Knapp Road together. They both remembered the day trip to Southend many years earlier.

Danny and Roberta moved around a lot after leaving Bow, moving to Poplar, Illford, Elm Park, Walthamstow, Marble Arch, Mayfair and then to Basildon. Finally in 2013 we moved up the road from Basildon to Vange. Not forgetting we bought a bungalow in Brandon, Norfolk.

We had to move from our flat in Vange, which was near to our daughter Deborah in 2013 as Bobbie became ill, and unfortunately fell down the stairs 4 times.

We just had to move but could not get a mortgage due to my age of 76 years.

Fortunately we were given a bungalow, next door to "The Barge".

Printed in Great Britain
by Amazon

39916979R00056